D1538866

# THE OUTDOORSMAN
## JOE FOSS

**By Joe Foss,**
**with Byron Dalrymple**

PHOTOGRAPHS BY ROBERT MATTOX

Published by Robert Halmi,
222 East 44th Street, New York,
in association with
the editors of TRUE

# ACKNOWLEDGEMENTS

*Many people who receive no credit have helped us mightily in the filming of our show. I think especially of wranglers chasing horses on frosty mornings, guides who have worked overlong and carried big loads besides, guests who have been patient with the demands of the TV camera and sound equipment. It's a long list of willing helpers and I doff my Stetson to each of them.*

*Flying in all sorts of planes and in some tough situations made this series possible. I am most appreciative of the efforts of American Airlines in getting us places and not losing our gear, and of Fairchild-Hiller's generosity in making a Sporter plane available to me.*

*Thanks also must go to the Remington Arms Company for its technical advice and the use of its products, and to the Shakespeare Company for its valuable suggestions and the chance to try out its latest fishing tackle in far places.*

*Finally, I particularly want to express my appreciation to the Liberty Mutual Insurance Company for its trust, encouragement and help.*

JOE FOSS

Copyright © 1968 by Joe Foss

Printed in the United States of America
at the Rockville, Maryland plant of
Fawcett-Haynes Printing Corporation

# CONTENTS

# INTRODUCTION

*I first got to know Joe Foss on a polar bear hunt in Alaska. Four of us, including Joe, had flown to Kotzebue with the ambition of downing our bears quickly, as Joe's time was quite limited. But the first chance Joe got to shoot a decent bear, he turned to one of my friends and remarked, "It's a beauty. You take it."*

*This sums up Joe Foss for me—he's a sportsman. As it turned out, we got our four bears in four incredible days and I am pleased to report that Joe shot the biggest. I have followed his career with increased interest ever since that happy day in 1960.*

*Robert Halmi I have known even longer. Bob was one of the pioneers in action photography in* TRUE. *He is the sort of guy who'd drive a burning car into a lake and take pictures inside as the water rushed in. His pictorial coverage of the outdoors in* TRUE *has long been outstanding.*

*So it was that when these two teamed up to film the TV series called "The Outdoorsman: Joe Foss" on hunting and fishing and conservation—with the accent on the latter—I silently applauded. And when I learned that their chief sponsor was the Liberty Mutual Insurance Company of Boston, an outfit that has long committed its entire advertising budget to promoting sportsmanship in the outdoors, I was even more pleased.*

*Joe Foss and Bob Halmi have taken on the world of hunting and fishing in a way that will enchant even the armchair sportsmen among us, and this book gives behind-the-scenes glimpses of some of their adventures.*

ROGER FAWCETT,
Publisher of TRUE, The Man's Magazine

# CHAPTER 1

# THE CHALLENGE
# OF WYOMING'S MIGHTY ELK

The Gros Ventre River country of northwestern Wyoming is a breathtaking sweep of raw and rugged wilderness. Here the brawling stream pitches down almost from the top of the Continental Divide, creasing the west slope and rushing headlong to join the Snake in its long and tortuous trip to the Columbia and finally to the Pacific.

Jim White (Wyoming's Director of Game and Fish) and I were maneuvering a Ski-Doo, a swift little motorized snow-sled, high up on a snowy slope. We were heading into the wind, whipping along with a plume of snow streaming out behind. The wind was bitter. The storm had been so severe that we'd had to give up hunting from horseback in our quest for a trophy bull elk. I was having a hair-raising thrill out of this novel way of hunting. This was, I reflected as I balanced precariously, the most off-beat elk hunt, to say the least, that anyone had ever been on.

There were thrills besides our mode of travel. The snow was driving the elk down from the high country. It seemed today that every elk in the entire Gros Ventre country was moving down the valley. We'd seen small groups of cows, a couple of straggling bulls with mediocre antlers, several spikes, more cows. Hardly an hour had passed without sighting at least a few animals.

I looked across a small, cuplike alpine valley and thought I detected a movement. I spoke to Jim

and he slowed and stopped. Over there a stand of stunted, twisted spruce thrust out of the deep snow. As we watched, a band of 12 elk streamed out of it. One of them, even at this distance, appeared to be a stunning old walloper of a bull.

Jim said excitedly, "That one ought to be good enough for you!"

I rolled off the Ski-Doo—and immediately sank almost to my armpits in snow. I got the Remington 7mm. up and started to look at the elk through the scope. For some reason I wanted to laugh. It just seemed to me that Jim and I must form the most preposterous hunter tableau that could ever be imagined. My heart was thumping—it always does when I get set to shoot. But I didn't know how I could hold steady on the brute from such a ridiculous stance as this.

Funny thing, almost every hunter of experience claims elk hunting is among the most difficult of big-game endeavors. A lot of elk are killed each season, to be sure. But of all the deer family these big fellows are among the most wary, and with a nature that is truly of the wilderness. Perhaps the easiest way to say it is that you can go deer hunting and spook a trophy buck, and follow it and it will as like as not be just over the next ridge, or the next. But get into elk country and spook a band and they may not stop for miles.

However, I guess I must have been rather lucky

in my elk hunting. I've seldom had much difficulty. For several years previous to this hunt, I had bagged my elk every season. I knew that it was not really that easy. And I also knew that just getting lucky didn't take away any of the excitement. In my opinion elk are one of the most exciting of all big-game animals.

It seems a little amazing that we call them by the name "elk" when actually they are not elk at all. When the English first settled in the Virginia colony they saw elk, which ranged far eastward then, and because the big animals looked somewhat similar to European moose, which were called "elk" by the British, this strictly North American animal was dubbed the same. The Indians here had called it wapiti. This was a Shawnee name. To this day many scientists still insist that we say "wapiti," but I cannot very well imagine any American hunter using the awkward term.

Although many elk in early days lived in some of the areas they still inhabit today, a great share of them were animals of the plains, and of the river bottoms throughout the plains. When, for example, Lewis and Clark trekked through the Northwest, they found no elk at all on the west slopes in what is now Montana. Records of early Army forts along the Missouri show that thousands of elk, taken both for food and hides, lived along the rivers of the plains in what is now eastern Montana. The herds ranged over almost two-thirds of the entire northern U.S., except for the Great Basin. There were elk in the Berkshires, in Michigan, elk far west on the Pacific coast.

It is well recorded that in earlier days elk were not very difficult to hunt. As plains and river-bottom animals, they were naive and no match for guns that could be shot at husky ranges. Even the Indians had little trouble killing them. Because hides were valuable as leather, hide hunters along the Missouri, for example, literally decimated the elk bands. Whole towns and forts were fed on elk meat. There is a record of a single shipment of elk hides from Fort Benton where one boat carried 33,000!

By the middle 1800's elk were drastically reduced over much of their range, and by 1900 this continuing slaughter had completely exterminated them from almost 90 percent of their original range. When you think how sharp they are today, how quickly they wind a hunter, it is difficult to imagine what those early bands must have been like. But at that, today's herds, even when hard hunted, still can show signs of fatal confusion if they are unable to wind or spot a group of hunters.

Elk, unfortunately, suffered at the hands of the Fraternal Brotherhood of the same name, too. At the turn of the century, every man who yearned for distinction wore a watch chain across his vest. If he was a member of the Elks, he adorned his watch chain with the canine tooth or "tusk" of the namesake animal. Incidentally, these are useless to the animal—they're found on the upper jaw, fairly well back. A good "tusk" is darkish brown and has distinct swirls, reminding one of the coloration of an agate marble.

When the craze was at its height, a good pair of teeth brought as much as $60. Even when the Isaac Walton League started feeding elk in Jackson Hole, Wyoming, during the winter, there were several men arrested for roping elk and pulling these teeth. It is estimated that at least a third of the decimated elk population was lost to the craze for this ornament. Often the entire animal was left to rot. I'm always trying to make excuses for man. But no matter how tough a man's economic situation, it's hard to imagine the kind of character who would earn money by jerking the teeth out of elk.

Elk are surprisingly big. And with their huge antlers they're deceptive. They look even bigger than they are. A bull will measure five feet at the withers. He may have a set of antlers that measure from the base around the curve a full 65 inches. Sometimes the distance between the beams, at their widest, is 50 inches or more. A really big bull may weigh when fat 1,000 pounds. Cows are smaller, averaging around 400, with average bulls about 700. A big bull may measure nine feet in length.

One of the mysteries of all time is how a bull elk can handle its immense rack when running through the brush. Sometimes they just don't seem to give a hoot. You'd think a locomotive had jumped the tracks. But on the other hand, three or four bulls when they want to can sneak soundlessly through jackpines so thick they'd give trouble to a man on foot.

From the rut on through the fall, a bull will generally be surrounded by a harem of cows. Bulls try to steal from each other's harems, and lone bulls that have lost out make raids. This also calls for fighting. The antlers of the bulls are vicious weapons, and the animals are tremendously powerful. Commonly a dressed carcass will show what a beating a bull has taken. There are rips in the hide, and big welts and bruises on the rib cage. Oddly, a yearling bull, which has only long spike antlers, can dish out more serious damage than a mature animal, if it works up its nerve to stand and fight. Not all spike bulls rut. But a few have been known to fatally puncture larger bulls.

Under certain circumstances it's easy to call bulls. The Indians made calls from wild parsnip, a bush-like plant with a stem that has stops in it, very much like a soft bamboo. They'd fashion a mouthpiece, plug the other end and cut a small slit in the top, like a child's whistle. They could make a very realistic noise with this. Even blowing across the top of a pop bottle will bring a bull that's really in full rut.

If you are above a bull, and his answering calls are getting closer, he'll often go to the sound of a small boulder rolled down the hill. On the South Fork of the Flathead River in Montana, a man was calling an elk and then ran through some brush to gain a vantage point atop a big rock. The bull he was calling ran toward the sound, probably thinking it was another bull, and went right over the top of the hunter, breaking his arm. Of course, this is an isolated case, but it's wise to be cautious when a bull is really on the prod.

After the rut is over, hunting has to be done by stalking or glassing. Most elk hunters in the mountains hunt from horseback, riding and looking for distant bands. This can be effective, but it is best to pause and spend an hour here or there on a high ridge where a large area of terrain can be watched. Unless one knows the terrain intimately, too much riding can spook elk out of the country.

We had several places in mind where we thought we could do an elk film for THE OUTDOORSMAN. I was especially interested in hunting the Jackson Hole herd. This was, and still is, one of the biggest herds in the country and has about the longest history of conservation behind it. I felt we should hunt as late in season as possible, for then the animals would be drifting down to lower country and would be more concentrated.

Before the little town of Jackson had good roads leading into it, and before Yellowstone Park to the north had become a "must" on every tourist's list, there was a large area of natural meadows here, irrigated by the Snake, Jenny Creek and the Gros Ventre River. There was an abundance of wild hay and much of this land was either bought or leased by the Isaac Walton League, an oldtime conservation organization that did much for fishing and hunting some years ago. Stacks of the wild hay were used to feed wintering elk that gathered in the foothills. After the species had reached a low ebb, the wintering program did a great deal to help rebuild the herd.

Although elk will graze on grass, their main staple is browse, that is, twigs, brush, and the bark of cottonwood and aspen. In their natural state, elk will winter along a river bottom, existing on the small willows that abound there. Highways and railroads, following as they often do the stream courses, have done much to diminish available browse. On some of the main rivers, which were wintering grounds for elk, a highway on one side and a railroad on the other have wiped out areas that once wintered thousands of elk.

Conversely, with advanced methods of game management and an accumulated knowledge, elk herds in numerous locations nowadays get too large and have to be controlled, or moved. Elk are actually very hardy creatures. There is not much of a predator problem to keep herds down. Numbers of hunting permits are annually based on surveys of herd size, health and calf drop. In many places, particularly in Montana and Wyoming, new elk herds have been started where no animals were originally present. Certainly today the elk is in no danger, and in places like Yellowstone, with no public hunting, there is—as all have read—a serious continuing problem of elk herds growing too large.

For our hunt we had gone out of the town of Jackson and followed up the Gros Ventre valley almost to the top of the Divide. On the other side, the east slope, there is the drainage of the Wind River. This entire region, on both slopes, is considered today and has been for many years, one of the finest elk hunting locations on the continent. There has long been a steady traffic up and down the Gros Ventre, over the Divide and into the Wind River range. The Yellowstone herd apparently mingles with the Gros Ventre herd, too, and the Gros Ventre group makes up in large part the herd that winters at Jackson. The number of elk is sometimes all but unbelievable. I recall having hunted on spring bear hunts in the Gros Ventre country when on a day's ride I could count several hundred pairs of shed antlers whitening on the low ridges.

When we arrived and set up camp, the weather was threatening. Scudding clouds whipped up snow flurries and you could practically feel the barometer acting up. We immediately began scouting to locate game in a place we thought we could cover properly with the camera. Tracks led every which way. Some elk were making a beeline for the lower country. Then in the very next draw all seemed headed up. I was surprised that bunches were so large. This was the latest in the season that I'd ever hunted. They were really ganged up.

From the undecided movement of game, we had fair warning that there must be a severe storm on the way. We weren't too worried, except for getting meat out with pack horses. Sometimes a fresh snow of some depth can be rough on horses carry-

**Bull elk become tame the moment they enter the national refuge at Jackson Hole.**

ing a load. They trail each other, wind up stepping in the same prints and get sore shins from the crust.

To say that next morning we had a tracking snow would be the understatement of all time. It was piled deep and it looked like more was coming. And, if not more, then plenty of wind to heap up tremendous drifts. I was worried that we had waited too long. Ken Martin, a state fish and game man, was guiding us, to make sure we got a good setup for the filming. He knew the country and did not seem to think we were in any danger. I was secretly glad we had gone no higher, for if the snow continued we'd surely have been hung up.

After a big breakfast we got our rifles and headed for the makeshift horse corral. It was tough walking just that short distance. I could not see how we could make much headway even with horses. I thought Ken was mulling this over and having misgivings, too.

Suddenly he said, "Boys, this is nonsense. We just aren't going to get anything done on horseback."

"What do you suggest?" I asked.

"Well," he replied thoughtfully, "if none of you has any objection I believe we ought to forget horses and fight this the modern way. After all, you fellows have a big job to do."

Somebody said, "What do you mean—'modern'?"

"Well," Ken grinned. "I'll just call Jim White, the Director, and get a snowmobile and a Ski-Doo up here." He paused and looked at us, and I think he knew he had everyone's consent. "There's a Forest Service phone about two miles away. I'll ride over to it." He mounted and left and we went back to hit the coffeepot, somewhat relieved, and also intrigued at this ingenious turn.

When Ken came back he said, "We're in luck. Jim was at the refuge. He'll be up in the snowmobile. And, he'll have a Ski-Doo along too. You get cattin' around on one of those and you'll sure see more country than any other way of travlin'."

When Jim arrived I was impressed by the equipment. I'd never ridden either kind of vehicle before. The Ski-Doo is really something. This type and several others have become extremely popular over the past several winters. This model was really a one-man rig, with a seat something like a motorcycle, and handlebars to steer a front ski. I could see why these machines were sweeping the country. Not only do they give a man complete mobility in snow that would require a pair of snowshoes to navigate, but they're great sport. They're a boon to the fish and game men, especially in a country such as we were in, because the welfare of a whole herd of elk—some 8,000 in the Teton National Forest herd—may depend on making sure none are stranded and cut off from the feed area.

I've known Jim White for years. He is one of the most knowledgeable elk men in the country. He really loves the animals. He has waged a war for their increase with such vehemence I've often thought it was a shame that such dedication couldn't be duplicated in other causes. Hunting with him is an education, and a privilege.

It was noon when we got started. But now our modus operandi was strictly twentieth century. Bob Halmi, Mark Dichter and I started out in the big snowmobile and Ken Martin followed on the Ski-Doo. Once in a while he'd leave the valley floor and make a sashay into the hills to check tracks and then, when he'd come boiling down, he'd leave a plume of flying snow while traveling a good 35 miles an hour. He'd turn the Ski-Doo by shifting his weight and the way he could weave through the timber was something.

As I said in the beginning, we were seeing elk regularly. There were bands here and there, and of course we were covering a lot of country. When we got within five miles of the top, we started running into them almost head on. Jim and I now took over the Ski-Doo and went up a side draw hoping to be able to find some elk that weren't traveling so diligently. I suppose I could have dropped off, hidden behind a tree, and picked off a good head. But so many bands were moving almost head to tail that they offered only chancy shooting. I wanted to find a bunch that was strung out.

The Ski-Doo, mounted on an endless, power-driven track, climbed like a tank, even with the two of us aboard. Mark Dichter and Bob Halmi, wearing snowshoes, had left the snowmobile, scenting action, and were puffing along behind us. We kept our pace very slow so they could keep up. I felt embarrassed, having it so easy, while they wallowed along. The top of the draw came into a wide depression, and I knew the flat place in the middle must be a small lake. We were now high enough so that this new snow was piled on top of earlier snows that had not melted. There must have been ten feet of it under us.

It was right at this point that I spotted the movement across the small valley and saw the dozen elk stream out of the thicket. Jim was excited when he got a look at the bull. And then I was off the Ski-Doo, wallowing around, getting my scope up and thinking what a preposterous sight we must make. I judge a trophy by beauty as much as by size. This one was in wonderful shape, and I knew it had at least six points each side. I decided this was it.

But now I began getting my shakes as usual. If I ever quit having them, as I've said many times, I'll stop hunting. I guessed the range at about 175 yards. I was going to have to shoot without a rest. But thanks to that little motorized sled, I wasn't puffing. I finally got the crosshairs settled on the heart region, sucked in my breath, let it half out,

and squeezed. The Remington hurled its sharp voice across the white mountains. As the echo rattled from ridge to ridge, the bull dropped and did not even quiver.

Bob Halmi and Mark Dichter were elated. They had recorded the entire scene. And now they helped us dress the bull and get the meat to the snowmobile. Be assured that was some job, in all the deep snow. Meanwhile, the sky was becoming overcast again. We wasted no time in heading back.

The next morning was cold and still. We hurriedly broke camp. We wanted to get down to the refuge to see if the elk were coming in. The snow squeaked as we moved along. The horses seemed happy that all they had to do was follow the trail broken by the snowmobile and Ski-Doo. We saw elk as far down as the old Gros Ventre Slide near Kelly. Jim felt sure they'd be in the fields by dark.

When we'd unpacked and hung the meat, Jim took us on a tour of the refuge. He showed us the cribs from which they feed pellets later and also the racks where they feed hay. Supplementing hay with pellets has made a big difference. The added protein has helped keep up the animals' strength and Jim felt sure the added expense was worth it.

I was amazed at the way the older animals came into the area. You'd think they knew its safety the moment they crossed the boundary. The same elk we'd seen the day before had been just as spooky as they could be, yet when they hit the meadows you could drive within 50 yards of them and they'd hardly look up.

The state of Wyoming is doing a tremendous job. Jim showed us with live models how they corral and earmark and brand elk for future information as to how far they range, and to gather information from recorded kills. They even go so far as to weigh them. Thus they have an accurate record of what they're accomplishing with the program.

I know that every hunter must have twinges when he realizes the extent of the work that's being done in conservation. Hearing about elk being handled like so many cattle must make him wonder if the game isn't getting too tame. It isn't. Many species seem to absorb man's help and still retain their sporting attributes when hunted.

Indeed, anything that's done to conserve game won't get a knock from me. And if you ever shoot a bull elk that's been tagged, I'd like to think you left that tag in the ear even when your trophy was on the wall. There's a great story and lots of effort behind such a tag—evidence of man's doing something to maintain the wild animals that provide his sport.

# CHAPTER 2

# GOOSE WONDERLAND
# AT REMINGTON FARMS

When we decided to do a show about goose shooting for THE OUTDOORSMAN, I immediately wanted to make it at Remington Farms, in Maryland. I had shot there in 1965 with Lee Wulff, and I thought the place was fabulous. Trying to describe Remington Farms to any average goose shooter, and especially to some old hand who has dug a pit in a Midwest wheat field when it was 10 below zero, is a sure way to get yourself called a liar. You just have to see the place to believe it.

The land is almost flat, and is surrounded on three sides by the waters of Langford Bay, and a small creek that flows into the Chester River. There has probably never been any place where so much time and money has been spent per acre of land and water surface on the pursuit of ducks and geese than on the eastern shore of Maryland. Remington Farms is a kind of exclamation point to all of it.

Almost all of the tillable soil is in corn. There are a couple of low areas back in the timber that have been flooded and put in millet. The place is sizable, but a 20-minute drive will place you anywhere on it. Just to the west of the main buildings is "the sanctuary." This is an area of possibly 30 acres of fresh water. It is bounded on the east by the road leading from the main buildings to the Old House, which is used for guests.

From the time the geese move south until the last ones have headed back north, the sanctuary is a haven for a great number that pass this way. At times as many as 20,000 birds are on it. But that's not all. Early in the year they are joined by as many as 15,000 pintails. There are swarms of mallards and black ducks. All the birds are used to seeing cars go from office to house. If you are in a car and keep moving, they'll barely flutter a feather. As dawn is breaking, the gabble from the sanctuary grows louder and louder. One who is nearby, listening, is certain he must be close to every goose and duck in the whole world. It just seems impossible to imagine so many birds.

Now then, there were other reasons in my mind, besides the vast number of birds available, for making our goose shooting film at Remington Farms. I wanted to give this exemplary place all the national exposure possible. For here so much had been done to solve some of the many serious problems confronting our waterfowl, and here much was being done to solve and to ward off the inevitable problems of the future.

Long before I had visited Remington Farms and seen Maryland's eastern shore in 1965, I had had a great desire to know more about this area. For it was here that meat hunters, market hunters and sportsmen had for many years been operating with such consuming passion that this, I felt, was a kind of educational center in the study of waterfowl and hunting them. I'd heard the area was great.

I doubt that any other locality in the world has had so much real estate, money and manpower totally devoted to duck and goose hunting. Wealthy men had bought scores of farms, planted thousands of dollars' worth of grain crops that had been gobbled up by the winged hordes. A tremendous amount of knowledge had been stacked up by these people and the resident biologists they hired, about how to handle these vast numbers of waterfowl.

Waterfowling has of course been pursued avidly in many places literally for centuries. It is one of the oldest forms of hunting, and by numbers of participants one of the most popular. Every corner of the world has its historic spot where some variety of waterfowl has been gathered, by one means or another. The sport, and the use of ducks and geese for food, are both ancient. There is evidence that the earliest inhabitants of North America used these birds as part of their diet.

In later centuries savages began to learn how to lure waterfowl almost as it is done today. For example, in a cave near Taos, New Mexico, archaeologists discovered a decoy fashioned of wood and straw which is thought to resemble a canvasback. The date of its probable use was fixed as prior to the time of the Conquistadors. To a modern hunter this conjures an amusing picture as he thinks of local nimrods and then sees them dissolve into naked Indians joking in a duck blind.

It was the market hunter who first tagged the Maryland shore as headed for waterfowling fame. On the Susquehannah flats was the great wintering ground of the succulent canvasback, one of the finest ducks for the table. Long before the Conewingo Dam was built, the Susquehannah made up the head of Chesapeake Bay. From Havre de Grace across to Northeast there was a broad expanse of water, brackish only when the wind blew from the southeast, where an abundance of wild celery grew. This was the mainstay of food for the diving ducks.

Here in fall literally thousands of them settled in—canvasbacks, redheads, greater and lesser scaups, ringnecks, whistlers, buffleheads. The entire area was designed by nature literally as a waterfowl paradise, as if this had been purposely done. Both sides of the great bay, all the way down to Cape Charles, were threaded by river mouths. Eastward across the peninsula—an easy flight for waterfowl—lay the bay born from the mouth of the Delaware. Indeed, nature had done the perfect job of mapping out a waterfowl heaven.

But it was not always to stay thus, even as perfect as it appeared. There were alarming low ebbs of birds, and unbelievable peaks, and these were happening long before man's damaging influences were felt. The duck and goose population has always had its limiting factors besides man. And of course there is much history that is hazy, that will never be filled in. Early records were mainly personal diaries. Not until Baltimore and Philadelphia offered enough consumers to draw market hunters to the scene did anyone more than mention in a memoir whether or not the sky "was black with winging waterfowl."

The eastern shore was slated for great waterfowl management and millions poured into it and into hunting, because it was such a compact and virtually perfect bird paradise, and it was to have a heavy surrounding human population. Out in South Dakota, which was my home, of course we had and still have tremendous duck and goose shooting. Our potholes and sloughs, in wet years, have been important nesting grounds. Depending on how controlled the shooting was, many a ranch could give a small group terrific shooting until the native birds headed south. Then, usually close to Armistice Day, we'd get what we called the northern flight. Great hordes of ducks, mostly mallards, would pour south, and if we had weather that would make them fly we'd have days, either near water or in the stubble fields, which were unbelievable.

Sometimes, when the metabolism of the birds causes them to really hit the feed, they can pour into places with an utter abandon that makes memories which last forever. We did all we could to hold water levels during dry years. And, with the influx after World War II of pheasant hunters, we even banned duck hunting for out-of-staters. Yet the weather, the water level, and the damming of the Missouri River all changed our hunting. It's still pretty good, but there were many things I'd like to have seen done in my home state.

When I was Governor of South Dakota I did get a few programs moving. I always kept thinking of the Maryland situation, about which I had heard a lot. There, I knew, federal, state and private funds had been and were being freely spent. I'd heard the hue and cry (which you always hear where the rich get the best hunting) that the "little man" didn't stand a chance. But I knew that it was just as true that many a wealthy sportsman had done more than his share to help *everyone* by his experimentation, by the very fact that he'd been successful in practices which made more game for the entire locality.

In the early Thirties, there was a very low ebb of ducks and geese. The eastern shore in those days had been pretty much a "diving duck" country both because of the great numbers of divers that stopped there, and because the locality had concentrated on hunting the species. Colloquial terms usually split the two main types of ducks as "dippers" and "divers."

The dippers—mallards, blacks, teal, widgeon, pintail, and gadwalls—have their landing gear set a little more forward and they can walk easily on land. Their natural way of feeding is in the shallows where they tip up and extend their necks down, cropping grasses within easy reach. This is not to imply they can't dive for feed but they prefer to eat in their natural manner, for which nature designed them. The "divers"—canvasbacks, redheads, scaup, ringnecks, and whistlers—will feed in 10 feet of water. And in their eastern wintering grounds the main staples of diet were marine plants growing on the tidal flats where fresh and salt water meet.

The "divers" are not too handy on land. They can, if pressed, get on and off a dry runway, but I'd hate to make the landings and takeoffs they make. To facilitate the diving, they have their gear set well back so that they get a full stroke with their big feet well back behind their tails.

In the early days the diving ducks gave the market hunter by far the best return for his efforts. The original method of hunting, which also appealed to the earliest "sports," was hunting on the flats from sink boxes or batteries. These were either one or two-man rigs. They were heavy metal boxes which floated flush with the water. Wooden shutters, weighted down by cast-iron decoys, kept the waves, if they were small, from lapping into the box. If a hard wind sprang up, that was the end of the hunting.

The rig was put out the night before a hunt, and as a rule the crew lived on a boat. Sometimes as many as 400 decoys, usually canvasbacks, were used, spread out to simulate a vast rick of feeding ducks. The sink box was placed in the middle of this huge rick. The gunner climbed in, the boat "tending" him pulled away, and when ducks started to fly, he'd lie down. If it was "one of those days" he could sit up and blast ducks which were practically taking his hat off. Because the rig was offshore, canvasbacks took an awful blasting. It was not uncommon for one gun to kill over 150 in a morning, go back to the boat, have lunch, then knock off another 100 in the afternoon. Even in those days a market hunter could get $2 apiece for canvasbacks. That was great wages. If he got a "sport" to do the shooting it was another $50 in the kitty.

At the first danger signals of the general decline of ducks 30 some years ago, the sinkbox was outlawed. "Bushwacking" took its place. It was done as follows. From a "mother boat," a hunter dressed in white would be sculled into the decoys after a bunch had landed. He could rear up behind a canvas blind around the prow, and blast away as the ducks took off. This wasn't very sporting shooting. Another method was to place a man in the water at the windward end of a big stool. He was dressed in white and in waders. With ice water up to his armpits, and chilling through his waders, this took a lot of stamina. It was called "body-booting" and it was sporting when decoying ducks came straight at you. But for marketing purposes nothing quite took the place of the old battery or sink box.

Ducks and geese began making a strong comeback in the early 1930's and up until the start of World War II. More and more people were buying land around the eastern shore, mainly farms on which they could hunt. But several influences now began to change the whole complexion of the sport.

First, the mechanical corn picker, which always leaves a few kernels on the ground, came into wide use. There was a decided increase in the numbers of migratory fowl using "stubble" fields. The combine appeared now for harvesting other grains. No longer were farmers standing bundles up to cure. With the binder going out and the combine in, waste small grain was left on the ground. Chemical fertilizer also influenced the picture. It became economical, and popular. It not only increased the acreage of crops but it made wheat and rye, planted in winter, a far stronger forage for geese in the spring. They headed north in much better shape than in former years.

In actual fact, geese had been something of a "side line" on the eastern shore. In the early Thirties, Ruliph R. M. Carpenter developed a farm on the Bohemia River. Its primary purpose was to hold geese. For several years the shooting he offered his friends came as close to being surefire as any goose shooting could be. When the weather was bad, adjacent farms had fine shooting, something which had been practically nonexistent until "Ruli" had gone to work. When the season was over, "Ruli" pampered his geese until they went north, convinced that many would return.

From immediately after the war until the middle 1950's, Maryland was in a constant uproar over baiting. The flats had lost much of their wild celery due to silt stirred up by the deepening of the canal connecting the heads of both the Chesapeake and the Delaware Bays. There was also the occasional dumping of the Conewingo Dam. A great deal of feed that held ducks was lost. There was nothing to draw them. With sink boxes outlawed too, the shooting was getting tough. And, waterfowl shooting was a real state industry. With market hunting greatly curtailed, more people were willing to spend more money to get a day's shooting. Many a farmer's blinds made him as much of an income as did his crops. So "guides" started dumping shelled corn in the water to attract both migratory fowl and the free-spending "sports."

There was nothing new about this method. Man had been controlling game, by way of their appetites, for ages. But the Maryland law stated "it is unlawful to bait within 250 yards of the blind" and the federal regulation at that time read that baiting was illegal "on or near the natural flyway." The battle was on.

If it had been possible to scan the whole eastern shore at dusk, one would have seen literally hundreds of boats putting out to "sugar" the ducks. Many would make a circle while someone inside poured corn down the toilet. The federal agents became increasingly tough. They used seaplanes and they could easily spot the corn on the bottom. Also, ducks feeding on bait, fed eagerly and in close formation. This was a dead giveaway. The federal enforcement people took to using helicopters. These whirly-birds for some inexplicable reason scare game. The federals broke the citizenry from baiting, but there's no doubt that the overall duck population of the area decreased.

I'd be the last one to feel qualified to argue pro or con, on the baiting question. I've heard some convincing arguments for both sides. But when it was a common practice, many a farm had built a "sanctuary," usually a freshwater pond that they never shot over but baited openly. In the middle 1950's these sanctuaries were loaded with ducks. Of course, they were mostly dippers because the divers prefer large bodies of water. But at the same time, guides were pouring grain in bays and the mouths of freshwater rivers and they were holding lots of ducks. These same guides, whenever their employers would foot the bill, were baiting after the season, too, and sending the birds north in fine shape.

Glenn L. Martin of aircraft manufacturing fame had a model duck and goose farm near Rock Hall, Maryland. He started working on a big sanctuary and later began breeding mallards. His idea was that if the duck population dropped to the "no shooting" point, he'd have a good idea of what could be done somewhat artificially. Here was a model farm, with shooting restricted to a certain number of days per week. It proved the terrific sport that could be had with a little work and

**High geese at Remington. Often they're quite low.**

knowledge, and were dedicated to wildfowl.

When Glenn Martin died in 1955, the Remington Arms Company, closely affiliated with the Du Pont Company (whose officers knew and hunted the eastern shore) bought the Martin farm as a promotional scheme. It was to be a place where they could take writers, their regional distributors, and others, all of whom would promote good will. The Remington people were genuinely interested in continuing the duck-breeding program, and they were also much interested in the goose shooting, which was becoming increasingly better.

When I was Governor of South Dakota I would have given anything to have had a couple of places like Remington Farms in the state! Here was the bankroll of a successful company behind experimentation, backing programs that either proved or disproved theories. Because the firm wanted people to go on burning Remington shells and using Remington guns, they were able to hit at problems affecting their market without being hampered by politics. Mind you, I think the Department of Interior is doing a good job. But they are bound by their very governmental role to consider the taxpayer and the voter. It is in my opinion hogwash to feel that anyone with the price of a hunting license and a duck stamp should be guaranteed good hunting, everywhere, in every state. It just won't work.

When we went down to Remington Farms in the middle of November 1966, the eastern shore goose population had reached a new high. Geese all along the Atlantic seabord had, in fact, been doing exceptionally well for many years. Just as with the ducks, the mechanical corn picker, the increasing use of chemical fertilizer and the many federal, state and privately owned sanctuaries have all been contributing factors to the increase of the geese. But in addition, their natural adaptation to man's pressure and assistance seems to have been better than that of the ducks.

Any of us who've hunted for 20 years remember the thrilling sight of how it once was, of geese decoying as though they just had to land right in the decoys. It's not so nowadays. They've become so "stool shy" that many a guide would rather depend on pass shooting. Geese have also become so flock and flyway oriented that they commonly travel in enormous armies.

The "great day" used to be when the birds were "trading"—smaller flocks flying in every direction, going to and from feed and water. Nowadays there's a general movement. Thousands will head out to the fields at the same time. One shot, causing this stream to deviate, and the shooter is all

through. Of course there's still the dream day, when it's spitting snow or there's a stinging, slanting rain beating from the southeast. But now it seems to take such lousy weather to make them handle well that a man can hardly shoot in it.

Along with their ability to figure out man's diabolical plans, geese seem to have been far smarter than ducks when it came to compensating for shrinking nesting grounds. Ducks will hang around a pothole which is drying up, catch botulism, and raise a clutch with three or four ducklings in it. Geese seem willing to nest near lakes and rivers, and even though they may prefer many of their ancestral nesting grounds, they still are able to make adjustments when places are drained, or there's a drought. The big birds simply move to where water is assured.

The sanctuary at Remington Farms is a perfect example of what geese, and many species of ducks, need. It offers them rest, an adjacent feeding area, and control over the amount they're shot. At the Farms, they hunt four times a week. The majority of the shooting could be termed "pass shooting." Blinds are all situated an equal distance from the sanctuary's shore—about 1,000 yards—and as the season goes on geese climb higher and higher, on the way out, but they still afford some shooting.

We flew down in the Heli-Porter and landed right on the farm. There were the McKees, Phyllis and Joe (shooting friends from Greenwich, Conn.), and Bob Halmi, Mark Dichter and myself. Our technical problems were rather simple compared to other shows we had filmed. But it seemed we were constantly hampered by poor light when we had the action. Also, and oddly enough, getting good sound was not as easy as we had anticipated. When the wind was quiet, Mark kept picking up foreign noises, of planes, trucks, farm machinery. It was also difficult to get sound on individual geese. In the general area there are several farms with huge flocks. At the time of day when all the geese were in the air, there was a general babble you'd imagine you could still hear as you dropped off to sleep.

The first blind we hunted from was a pit blind, probably the most widely used type everywhere, and it was well built. Five guns had ample room in the cement block fortress, and the flop-over-top, flush with the ground, concealed us from the birds above.

Benny Johnson, a typical eastern shore waterman, guided us and he was an exceptional caller, using nothing but his voice. We concentrated on killing geese only for the camera. This made it far sportier. But in the pit blind we had trouble with

The sanctuary at Remington Farms holds ducks and geese by the thousands.

Clark G. Webster

our timing. Getting the top flopped back and taking the geese when they were closest was difficult.

It was in the pit-blind I became convinced that the birds were really smart about decoys. Benny had put out a fine-looking stool. The decoys were freshly painted, full-bodied, some with their necks down in a feeding pose, and they were scattered around so that they looked natural. Even the first bunch of geese that passed over, however, knew exactly where they were going. The fact that others —our fakes—supposedly had found feed on the route, didn't faze those in the air. I've listened

to geese enough so I recognize a flying bunch when they talk to those on the ground. There was none of this chatter. The flyers were on their way. It was easy to see that one of their past weaknesses, decoying to others, had been overcome. The species, I surmised, thereby had a new lease on survival. They had learned from man. They had been "conditioned."

The first morning we shot, our set-up was lucky. The wind was at our backs, there were two flyways of geese going. One was almost directly overhead, the other to our right, heading due north. We faced west, which placed the morning light just right for the camera, and Benny seemed able to bend flocks a little closer with his calling. At first, however, even with the perfect conditions, we were smothered with confusion.

We'd pop up, hit our heads on the "flop-top" and be sitting down again just as Benny would throw it open for us to shoot. After a couple of abortive attempts at timing, however, we did carve three out of a bunch. Exactly as it says in the books, we "folded them." Bob Halmi was in a blind behind us, dug purposely for him and his camera. As everyone knows, movie cameramen never applaud. But in this case even Bob, the most non-committal of Hungarians, gave what was assumed to be grunts of approval. Both Phyllis and Joe McKee are excellent shots, yet it was some time before they—and I—mastered getting on the same goose the camera was on. After about an hour we decided to give them a rest and try a different spot in the afternoon.

It is weird the way geese decide when it's time, either morning or afternoon, to take off. The tempo and pitch of their gabbling changes; then the first bunch moves out. Slowly the traffic builds, finally the air above the sanctuary looks as though there would have to be some collisions. There are always a few coming back and to avoid hitting others they do the darnedest dipsie-doodles. We caught some of these in slow motion. They tip from level to past 90 degrees, and often whip back 180 degrees so that their wings are perpendicular to the ground. When the air was still, or if there was fog, they'd make a noise like tearing a sheet.

The combination of being so close to game and still having sporting shooting is unique. I'd say that the men behind this outfit couldn't be too highly praised. Joe Linduska, a biologist who was there at the time, and Clark Webster, who majored in botany at George Washington University, were the biologists in recent years, and there have been other people deserving credit before them. But my hat is off to Glenn Martin and the Remington people, who had the foresight to stay with the waterfowl program. We hunted two and a half days and I'd say we could have had our two-goose limits on any of the days in the first 20 minutes. We tried the ducks. Perhaps half of them were mallards raised on the farm. The rest were wild mallards, pintails, and the occasional black. It was bluebird weather. Only odd bunches moved.

One morning we set up on the edge of the farm where it juts into a part of Langford Bay. Just as the sun came up, the ducks excited us with natural "trading." Several bunches spotted the decoys and came in, as I always say it, "with their hats in their hands." There is no thrill like the moment a duck slows its wing beat and makes up its mind to sit down. Watching a duck through a peephole in a blind and then taking it the moment you feel is just right is the biggest thrill any hunter can have.

Our last evening there we were trying with the camera to perfect some "shoot downs." This means putting the camera right on the bird as it is shot. This is not easy. To do it well the cameraman has to quickly establish the bird he is following in his viewfinder, and then the "gun" has to wait until the cameraman gives him the verbal "ready, aim, fire!" Joe and Phyllis were getting to be old hands at this movie-shooting. Benny, the guide, seemed to be in extra fine calling voice and the geese, although they crowded the fading light, were overflowing the sanctuary and had yet to feed.

Our blind was on the back edge of a strip of standing corn and we had far too much equipment crammed into a blind that two men would ordinarily shoot out of. As long as I live I'll never forget that evening. To the west there was a film of haze that made the sun a bright orange-red. There'd been a dead period with utterly no movement. Then one single goose appeared. Following, over the corn, we could see one bunch, and another. Hundreds were suddenly coming directly toward us. We'd decided that in spite of the fast-waning light we'd let the flight build a little so there'd be noise behind us which we hoped would hold them on course.

It doesn't happen often in game photography that there comes a moment of extreme elation when everything works perfectly. This was one such moment. We could hear the camera whirring. We shot. Three fell. It was crystal-pure, whole drama.

Joe, Phyllis and I stayed in the blind long after we'd run out of light. The big, majestic birds beat their way over us out toward the field in which they'd feed that night. Bunches joined other groups over our heads until endless "V's" were passing against the lovely orange light.

Finally we left the blind. As if a documentary film had been shown us, I could in retrospect piece together all the work that had been done. I'd seen the truly astounding results of a great experiment. The geese—and the ducks—I knew would be safe as long as we had dedicated people such as those who had stubbornly fashioned this wonderful sanctuary on Maryland's eastern shore.

**Mallards are an always welcome bonus at Remington**

Above, Joe Foss, with Mr. and Mrs. Joe McKee on his right, at Remington Farms. Below, flight of geese swing over their blind. Opposite, Joe Foss warms up during Wyoming elk hunt.

Going was tough
toward elk camp
in driving snow of
the Gros Ventre country.

Ken Martin and
Joe Foss, (left)
track elk through
the snow. Bagging
this big beautiful
trophy was a
triumph for hunters
and photographer Halmi.

Our Fairchild-Hiller "Sporter" carried the whole crew
and all our gear. It was ideal for our shooting sched
because, being a STOL-type of aircraft, it could take off
and land in small areas. For example, we flew on and off
of an Alaskan glacier, the top of a Hawaiian volcano and into
a small clearing in the jungle of British Honduras.

# CHAPTER 3

# HOW TO PICK THE GEAR FOR THAT DREAM TRIP

People are constantly asking my advice about what equipment they should take on hunting and fishing trips. Many know that I have made scores of long trips of this kind, and seem to feel that I must have evolved some sort of system that makes it easy and rather automatic as to what to take and what to leave at home.

This is not actually true at all. There is no one rule, no single set of equipment that will fill all needs in all places at all times. However, to help all readers as much as possible, I will try to put down here a few things that I have learned over the years about selection of equipment. I believe it will make the chore of getting an outfit together at least somewhat easier.

The first consideration is, of course, what your budget will stand. Even so, there is such a welter of items to select from today that compromises can be made to keep a good outfit, for any usage, within a reasonable budget. A cardinal rule nonetheless should be that "you get what you pay for." A sleeping bag selling at $10 cannot possibly be a very good one, and it just may be so poorly made that you'd be better off with blankets taken from home. Try to stretch your dollars, but don't see how cheaply you can put together an outfit. If you are going to skimp, do so where a product of poorer quality is not vital to your health or comfort.

The next consideration has nothing to do, actually, with specific items to make up an outfit. It concerns *how you will travel*. For example, let us suppose that you own a station wagon and you are going to go on a fishing and camping trip to a place like Yellowstone Park, or outside the park on north of West Yellowstone along the Gallatin River. Here, in either place, pavement runs right beside the rivers where you will fish. You will not even get off it in Yellowstone to pitch your camp, and up the Gallatin you will drive barely a few car lengths off the highway and camp under the pines beside the river. There are thousands of such places all over the U.S. In planning such a vacation, and with an ample amount of room in your vehicle, it really doesn't make any difference how *much* equipment you take. Pile it in. Why not? If you want to try out six different fly rods, there is room in the wagon.

Conversely, don't stow up with a deluge of assorted gear at some outfitter's headquarters, expecting to be packed up to a scattering of glacial lakes at 11,000 feet, at the end of a 20-mile horseback ride. As an example, I have a wonderful and enormous sleeping bag that is so comfortable I hate ever to be without it. But it is so large and heavy and bulky that I would hardly expect to pack it on horseback up into the mountains. Far better is a small, compact, and very light down bag I have that can be rolled into a small packet, then fluffed up to become suitable for near-zero use. All equipment, from fishing rods to guns, etc., should be selected for pack trips with lightness and compactness in mind. This kind of trip requires real planning in order that you may be comfortable yet not wallowing in a welter of unnecessary gear.

The next consideration in planning an outfit is *where* you will use it the most. I mean by this at what altitude, how far or near civilization and supply points, in what climates. It is a simple matter to outfit for a consistently warm area, such as a trip along the Mexican border during spring or fall. You know that the only temperature extremes you are likely to meet will be from warm to hot. But when you go, up into the mountains in Wyoming on a spring bear hunt in June, you will almost certainly meet several extremes of weather—rain or snow, freezing temperatures at night, perhaps midday temperatures of 80 degrees, with intermittent rain squalls. Clothing and boots and other items must be carefully chosen to cover these extremes.

They must in addition be the more carefully chosen dependent again on how you travel. If by station wagon, take warm weather clothing, cold weather clothing, rain gear. You've got plenty of room. If by horseback or 4-wheel-drive into the wilderness, compromises must be made. The mark of the experienced outdoorsman is how small and light a "bundle" he can take along under such conditions and still be comfortable at all times.

The consideration of *where* must have great influence upon all sorts of items of equipment besides clothing. Let me give you some examples. On an ordinary camping trip that will be near supply points, quite obviously an ice chest or cooler is a standard item. On the other hand, it is useless on a pack trip, unnecessary in the extreme, and too big and bulky to bother with. Foods for a pack must be selected that do not require much, or no, refrigeration.

A big flash lantern that runs on batteries is very handy in a camp near supply points. But it is bulky to pack up into the mountains, and becomes as useless as an electric stove once its battery gives out. A small flashlight should certainly be taken, with some spare, fresh batteries. But if a large light is considered necessary, then a standard gasoline lantern with a single gallon of gasoline in a rugged can is far better that battery lights.

This same sort of situation exists with much of the new butane equipment. Butane stoves and butane lights are excellent. But they are for use in civilized situations, and in situations where positive supply points are close at hand. A butane light or stove up in the mountains or the back country may as well be thrown away when the gas runs out. Also, the tanks are too heavy and bulky for such use. I think from these examples it should be evident how to make choices about such things.

Now let's get down to some specifics. Make up for your individual needs a small and compact case of some sort—perhaps even a canvas zipper bag that can be pushed easily into your duffle bag. In this will go basic first-aid materials, toothpaste and toothbrush, aspirin, an extra set of boot laces, a small jackknife as a spare, a small flashlight, bug repellent, a couple of plumber's candles, matches in a waterproof container—etc. I'm sure each individual will have various small items he uses or feels he needs, and there will be differences of opinion. But this basic kit you can work out on trip after trip, adding or subtracting as needs are felt. I put in a few silly things like a scattering of paper clips (handy to fix all sorts of things), a small bottle of glue such as Elmer's, some rubber bands.

Make up such a kit so it will cover both hunting and fishing. Keep it always supplied and always with you. For instance, you want some liquid plastic—for patching waders—or else regular wader patches. Don't keep adding so much that it becomes too much of a conglomeration and so that a lot is never used. A snake-bite kit should go in here, too, but be taken out and carried in your pocket when hunting or fishing in any area where snakes may be even mildy abundant. Along with this kit will be your razor. Letting one's beard grow on camping or packing trips, incidentally, is in my opinion a most uncomfortable thing to do.

When you start selecting clothing, here are a few pointers. In areas where temperature changes are drastic, take a couple of light wool shirts, a suit of down or Dacron underwear, and a Nylon rain suit. This combo keeps you warm and dry with the least possible bulk. The down underwear can also be worn in your sleeping bag as an "extra bag" if needed. If the weather will be consistently cold, down (or Dacron) and wool will be your best bets. A heavy wool jacket will soak up a tremendous amount of snow, and a good deal of rain without wetting you, if you get caught out. But always, on horseback or elsewhere, keep that Nylon parka and pants at hand. They can be rolled up and stuffed into a game pocket, or your hip pocket for that matter. But be ready!

There are many good outer garments with shells made of treated poplin or other such materials. These are fine, but bear in mind that they are noisy when you must make a quiet stalk. Wool is quiet, and good wool wears for many years. Of course, there are situations where you don't want wool. One is in desert going where there is much cactus and thorn brush. I often wear, in such walking or riding, hunting pants with leather or canvas facing, and economical cotton shirts, with a light jacket of some hard-finish material. I would not ever ride horseback in brush country or thorn or cactus country without chaps. If you will do much riding, get yourself a pair. Have them made, if possible, to fit you properly. Also, in desert hunting or travel, wear long sleeved shirts. Short sleeved ones are not a good idea. You may burn too badly. Long sleeves also ward off insects and thorns to some extent. And you can always roll up long sleeves if necessary.

Hats, either in desert or mountains, should in my opinion be wide brimmed, and except in rare cases be of good felt that can get wet and still dry out without shrinking or losing shape. In snow country a cap with earflaps is a good idea. This is obvious. And in very hot desert travel, a straw hat beats felt.

When you get down to selecting boots, you can have all kinds of problems. But actually good common sense should settle most of them. For many types of hunting or fishing I like boots only 6 or 7 inches high. But in grassy country they are "seed catchers" of the worst sort. By and large, boots of standard height around 9 inches are the best compromise, unless you wish to have several pairs.

There are certain leather boots marketed today that are guaranteed waterproof. Such boots are excellent for all-round use. Many boots can be had nowadays either insulated or not insulated. Very heavy insulation defeats its purpose by making the boot too bulky. Moderate insulation can be worn even in warm weather without discomfort, and can be a good compromise. Boots that are glove-leather lined are very comfortable. None of the boots I am describing is cheap. There aren't any really good cheap boots, period.

The sole of the boots you wear is one of the most important items of your equipment, and too often not even considered by the camper, hunter or fisherman. Leather soles are abominable. They slip on grass and rocks, and often on wet going. Certain types of synthetics are terribly dangerous because they slip on wet surfaces. One tremen-dously popular brand of lightweight boots and shoes several years ago had such a sole—it was fine on dry going, but would kill you on wet rocks.

Good, tough composition soles that adhere to all surfaces are the only kind to have. In thorn country such as where numerous mesquites and ratamas grow, such soles should be of the cushion type, that is, thick enough so tough thorns will not penetrate clear through. A husky mesquite thorn of large size is a wicked and exceedingly tough instrument of torture. Nowadays many boots are advertised with "mountain-climber" soles. These deeply scored and hobbed composition soles are questionable for average sportsman use. They gather mud and grass in wet going. So, in-cidentally, do the supposedly excellent "self-cleaning" ripple types. They stick badly in a stir-rup and could be dangerous. My advice is to avoid them for all but the most rugged of alpine going.

I have already mentioned sleeping bags. Use as big and bulky a bag as you like when trans-port is no problem. But for back-in going, cut it down to a compact type. The mummy style used by climbers and back packers is the most com-pact type you can get. The down underwear pre-viously mentioned makes it a double bag in a pinch. An ordinary large sheet of heavy vinyl makes an excellent ground cloth or emergency rain protection for your bag. It can be folded and packed in very little space.

Mattresses are sometimes a perplexing problem. Good sound comfortable sleep is important to a hard-going outdoorsman. The standard air mat-tress has been with us many years. It has served well. But it has many drawbacks. One is that it must be pumped up, and deflated after use. An-other is that air mattresses do get punctures, or leaky valves, and they can let you down—liter-ally. Cheap plastic air mattresses costing a couple of dollars will do for a brief campout via station wagon. But they are an invitation to discomfort on a pack trip for they puncture or pinhole too easily. Don't skimp on quality here.

In the field of kitchen equipment I have al-ready touched lightly. Here are a few further sug-gestions. Shy from aluminum or tin cups. Hot tea or coffee in them burn your lips; Use plastic or enameled-metal cups. Don't get an idea a belt hatchet will chop your firewood. Take a good ax. There are several small folding saws that pack in very small spaces and unfold to do an excel-lent job on wood of modest size. The old-fash-ioned sheepherder's stove is one of the best pack-in and back-country bets going. Of course, you'll have to rustle the fuel to stoke it. Single-burner "pocket type" stoves are okay for backpack uses. But in general cooking over a campfire is a superior means. The little stoves are just too dinky to get much grub going for a regular camp. Again, if you have no restrictions on packing room, then the standard gasoline stove is still today the best bet you can find for all-round usage. In fact, a two-burner gasoline stove and a gallon of fuel can be packed with a pack string up into the mountains, or via canoe or small power boat into the lake country, and serve well for a couple of weeks in making meals quickly and efficiently.

Probably I am asked more about tackle and guns than about any other items of equipment. I feel it is useless to discuss guns, for every rifleman or shotgunner has his very deep prejudices and these are hard to put down. I would simply say that I feel many hunters do go overgunned for average game nowadays. And some select a rifle for a mountain hunt, for example, that is a real cross to bear when you have to carry it day after day. For such work, a short-barreled rifle powerful enough to do what you are intending to do with it is what you should think about. I do all my TV work with just two Remington Model 700 rifles, one a .375 H & H, the other in 7 mm. Remington magnum caliber.

In fishing tackle, there is more room to make suggestions. Ninety percent of fishermen today are overburdened with vast collections of tackle they do not need, and seldom use. Some of them are what might be called "collectors" and certainly there is no harm in that, if you can carry it around. But the one thing back-country travel teaches you, whether you do it by horse or plane or canoe, is that you can get the job done just as efficiently with a scant percentage of the tackle the average angler is inclined to take with him.

Consider first the matter of lures. A fly fisherman should take a good selection of *sizes,* from very small to flies of fair size. But it he takes these in shades running from white to black, that is, through the browns and grays, and nothing else, he will be astonished at how good a job he can get done under almost any circumstance. The matter of patterns, by name, is not really very important. The size of a fly, and its shade from light to dark, are the most important considerations. For trout fishing, all of this applies to dry flies, wet flies, including nymphs. Although streamers are very productive at times, by and large a compact collection of drys and nymphs will get the job done. It is in my view more important to have *enough* of each size and shade rather than a vast number of individual patterns.

Much of this applies to warm-water fly fishing, too. If I were going to fly fish in salt water, or in fresh water for such species as bass and panfishes, I would dote on yellows, whites, pinks, orange, with a few blacks and browns thrown in. This goes for bass bugs as well as streamer flies and all other types. These colors—in varied *sizes*—will do it under almost all conditions, if the fish will hit at all.

Let's say now that you are going into the north country, or the mountains, and you are not a fly fisherman. You will use either spinning or casting equipment. You are in a situation where you can't very well take along a huge tackle box. What about lures? Very simple. Forget all the plugs and the bulky lures. You will be fishing for trout, or else for pike, walleyes, smallmouth bass. These in the north country and the mountains will be the main species. A collection of spoons is all you need. Absolutely all. These, again, should have great variety of size. They should also cover in color the following: bronze, copper, silver, plus crystal finishes in these, plus red-and-white, black-and-white, perch and frog finishes. If you can't catch the species mentioned with this selection, you can't catch them at all, and you may quote me!

To facilitate packing this spoon collection, try the following: take several small boxes of treble and single hooks, a box of split rings. Take the hooks off all the spoons. Now package the hook-less lures in a small, compact container, even a small canvas kit. They cannot become tangled, and you put on hooks as you use the spoons. If you are catching fish fast and releasing them, use single hooks. They're easier to remove.

What, now, about rods and reels? I take my Shakespeare spin reel, and fly reel, with several spools for each containing various lines. The fly fisherman should put a sinking line and a floating line on different spools, and possibly one with sinking tip, on which the body of the line floats. The spin man takes a reel of substantial strength and size, and carries with it spools loaded with line of varying weight—several of them. I'd say for back-in trips a spare reel should also be stowed away, in either case.

In rods there are many opinions. But if room and weight and general size of the package are a critical factor, then the so-called back-pack rods built by several makers nowadays are just what you want. These come in fly, spin, and casting styles, and most measure a mere 24 inches when taken down and cased. They solve the horseback problem beautifully, and most of them are very good little rods, short but quite powerful.

My favorite is Shakespeare's Jet Set—a four-in-one pack rod that is a spinning rod, a fly rod, a casting rod and a spincasting rod all rolled up into one. Its seven pieces fit into a small vinyl case. With the Jet Set and three or four reels I'm ready to tackle just about any kind of fishing—anywhere.

I would certainly have a spare rod along, regardless of what type of fisherman I was. I like the white Shakespeare rods, incidentally, because they photograph well. You may too.

There are thousands of words that could be added here to give minute details about equipment. But I think I have made my overall philosophy clear about putting together an outfit for *you*. Consider *where* you will go, and *how* you will go, and how long you will be gone. Few persons stay more than a week or two in the wilderness. A very few make a trip of a month. You will be surprised, if you really start cutting down, how light you can go and still have everything you really need.

If you aren't going to go "back in," then cart along the whole house if you must. But just bear in mind that the gents who nowadays take their portable TV's and record players, and power generators to run their toasters and drink mixers, aren't really camping, or roughing it. They might as well stay home. Let's be comfortable while camping, but let's know where to draw the line. Go light. You'll enhance your enjoyment if you don't try to take all the "wild" out of the wilderness!

But first you have to get there and whenever possible I travel by air. Show watchers know I use a Fairchild-Hiller specialized craft called a Heli-Porter. This plane is amazing in its ability to get into and out of tight places. Often I've landed it in less than five times its 35-foot length.

And talk about carrying a load! I could stuff a one-ton moose whole into the plane and take off from or land on a cleared field no more than 500 feet long.

The Heli-Porter's flight characteristics make it a snap to fly—you don't have to be a command pilot to hustle this baby. She'll comfortably hold eight passengers, including me, and with three-abreast seating can accommodate 11. The tracked seats are easy to remove should you need space for cargo stowage.

This plane cruises easily at 150 mph. at 10,000 feet but can loaf along at only 42 mph. She stalls at a low, low 30 mph. with power and flaps. What's more— But, shucks, I just meant to talk about *flying*.

Have you considered using a commercial airline lately when planning a hunting, fishing or camping trip? If not, you should know that in the summer of 1965, the airlines quit charging you for baggage *weight* on domestic flights and instead began charging by the number of *pieces of baggage*. Extra baggage costs only a dollar or so per piece, regardless of weight. Suddenly you could fly to some far place—save days of auto travel—and arrive fresh with all your gear.

Furthermore, airlines like American—which I have had good luck using whenever I fly "commercial"—aren't stuffy about carrying a sportsman's guns.

Take-down type guns should be just that—taken apart in two pieces; and you must remove the bolt from a bolt-action rifle. These are the basic regulations. Tell the guy quietly at the weigh-in counter what you have (he may want to check to see that the bolt is out, for instance) and chances are he may arrange to have your pet rifle —carefully sighted in at home—carried into a forward cabin compartment for hand delivery to you upon arrival.

American is truly an airline that understands outdoorsmen and caters to them. Suppose you want to take Old Rover on a bird-hunting trip across the country and you don't have a travel kennel. American will provide one that'll handle most dogs weighing up to 70 pounds for only $12.75 and it's yours (or Rover's!) at the end of the trip.

Were you aware of the American Sportsman Club (101 Outdoors Building, Columbia, Mo. 65201)? It publishes booklets showing a wide variety of fishing, hunting and outdoor trips across the country, with tour prices, trip fares, etc. Get on the mailing list—you may be headed somewhere soon and should be packing your fishing rods or guns.

American will even rent you one of those big, plush family campers out West—the kind you can live it up in with shower, air conditioning, comfortable beds, the works.

The big thing for us about flying is the tremendous amount of time it saves us. Often we work so hard on filming the various shows that we look forward to a longish flight—you can stretch out and relax, collect your scattered thoughts and even draw a leisurely breath or two before the next struggle.

As you can see, I get carried away on the subject of flying. I've done it most of my life and it gets easier all the time. For the sportsman, it means precious days afield that are now available in no other way.

# CHAPTER 4

# THE FISH
# I LOVE TO HUNT
## By Henry Shakespeare

I stood on the foredeck of the 18-foot open boat straining my eyes to penetrate the 14 feet of rippled salt water that stretched away in greens, blues and mottled bottom colors in all directions. Hard at my right shoulder—so close we cast just one shadow —stood my guide, equally intent, peering silently into the water.

He saw them first. Slim black shadows, three of them, gliding directly toward the bow from 50 feet to our left.

"Cast straight off the bow, not too far," he barked urgently. "Let it sink to their depth. Retrieve fast—now slow down. Slower! Keep it coming, but just barely move it!"

I retrieved the tapered fly line by inches with my left hand, barely twitching the orange streamer. Out of the corner of my eye I saw the three shadows, bigger now, on a collision course with the fly. Not 20 feet out from the boat the lead fish let the fly pass its nose four inches away, then turned and followed silently almost to the boat. A black maw opened; the fly disappeared. I waited a fractional second, then lifted the rod tip sharply.

Wow!

The slim black shadow became a slab-sided silver monster as it broke water 30 feet from where it had taken the fly. Head shaking and body almost bent double, it jumped seven feet straight up out of the water and fell with a jarring splash. I hit the fish hard then. Three quick hook-setting strikes against a bony mouth. And all you can do was hope the needle-sharp hook found a spot to sink home.

The huge fish is out of water again, loose fly line gone from my stinging left hand, and the big fly reel's drag starts to zing. And again it jumps! Then it's coming toward the boat—faster than I can turn the reel handle to retrieve line. Another jump. The line is tight now, no slack. Once more. Look out! Here comes the fly, shaken from the steel-hard jaw and straight as a dart it shoots to rattle harmlessly off the boat hull.

That's the tarpon. A fish to stalk.

Now join me in the same Florida waters, but out on the "flats," shallow areas where the water is often only knee-deep.

The guide poles silently with a 20-foot fiberglass pole that eases his shallow-draft boat over the water without disturbance. Again we search the water, using Polaroid sunglasses that filter the glare and make it possible to see beneath the surface twice as easily as with the naked eye.

My guide holds up his hand and leans on the pole to stop our forward motion. He points and I see the silver-black forked tail sticking straight from the water 30 yards from the boat. It waves gently, then disappears. As the guide points again, I make out the gray shapes in the water, closer now. How tricky they are to keep in sight.

The spinning rod and reel have been ready in my hand, reel bail cocked for a cast. I flip the pink quarter-ounce jig well out ahead of the path of the cruising fish and let it sink to bottom. As a tiny ripple betrays the presence of the school six feet from the jig, I lift the rod to raise the lure a foot from the bottom, then let it drop. When I lift it again the line tightens and I set the hook.

Now listen to the prettiest song in fishing: the soprano aria of a well-set spin reel drag pitted against the 100-yard run of a blurred gray racer, headed for deeper water. Rod butt pointed toward the fish and held high over my head so the line won't snag on the bottom, I hang on waiting for the steady strain of bowed rod and six-pound monofilament to slow my prize down.

When the fish stops at last I retrieve a few yards and it's off again. Three more runs and 10 minutes later the guide slips his net under an exhausted eight-pounder and gently releases the fish.

That's the bonefish. A fish to stalk. . . .

The title of this chapter may have surprised some fishermen. *Hunting* for fish. But the tarpon and the bonefish—under the circumstances I've described—are just two fish species that may be actually hunted.

The Florida Keys, with much of the fishing based on the towns of Islamorada and Marathon, present fish-hunting opportunities that are probably unique in this country. Besides tarpon—at certain times of year—and bonefish, the permit and redfish (or channel bass) are also stalked in a similar manner near the Keys. The clear, shallow water and trained guides, who know the habits of the quarry, make it possible to enjoy this most fascinating type of angling.

This combination fishing-hunting is the most exciting sport I've found in an angling career that has taken me to three continents and several oceans.

Hunting for fish, however, I think must be carefully defined. In my definition of the sport, two elements have to be present: 1. You must be able to see the fish in advance. 2. You must present the lure to a particular fish or school of fish.

I think of fish-hunting in the Keys as closely akin to duck hunting from a blind. The boat is the blind, and (in the case of tarpon "hunting") it's usually "staked out" on a bar or underwater ridge. That is, the boat is tied to the pole which has been shoved firmly into the bottom.

The tarpon are patiently watched for, the angler standing at the ready, always prepared to cast.

The fish, like ducks, come by either as "singles" or more usually in "flocks," or schools. The angler, like the hunter, picks out just one target and concentrates on intercepting it with his lure. Just as the gunner figures lead, angle and elevation to get his shot charge to meet the duck in flight, so the fisherman must figure speed, depth and angle of the approaching fish so that the fly or lure comes within scant inches of the swimming tarpon.

Even when actively feeding, the Keys tarpon will not usually move any great distance to chase a lure. But when presented with what looks like a choice morsel of food that's ready for the eating if it just opens its mouth, the Silver King will usually strike. As I explained, however, the strike is only the beginning. You must first set the hook —no mean trick given the tarpon's rocky mouth —then withstand as many as six or eight violent jumps and finally wear down a fish that commonly weighs well over 100 pounds. It's a humbling and unforgiving kind of fishing with light tackle.

One of the best and most practiced fishermen at Islamorada, Ted Williams, figures on one tarpon brought to the boat for every four strikes he receives. (I think the odds for the average fisherman would be more like one in eight.) I kept track of one angler during a recent five-day fishing stint—he had strikes from 23 tarpon, had 12 of these on for one jump or more, and caught *just one 50-pounder,* which he released. This on spinning tackle, with 15-pound-test line, which gives the fish plenty of advantages.

Personally I favor fly tackle for tarpon stalking; I think it produces more strikes, more hooked fish and the fly rod is a good fighting instrument for putting the pressure on a big fish.

In the case of the bonefish, stalking comes more into play. Bonefishing might be likened to hunting deer with a rifle.

You spot your "game" first—either swimming or "tailing," as I described. A bonefish with its tail out of water is feeding on crabs or other crustaceans in very shallow water, so shallow that when it reaches down to pick up the food the tail comes clear of the surface. At other times the bonefish are seen "mudding," stirring up the bottom in their search for food, but not actually breaking water with their tails.

Your guide moves the boat as quietly as possible within "shooting" range of the target. One thump of a foot against the deck or even an extra hard push of the pole against the bottom and you've spooked the fish—just as a cough or sudden breeze from hunter to deer will send those

I heft a lusty rainbow, one of my fly rod favorites.

animals hightailing it into the woods.

If you do get into casting range of the bonefish you're pursuing, you must lead the target precisely. Cast too close to the swimming fish and you'll scare them; too far and they won't see your offering. And once a "bone" picks up your lure you have your hands full. No jumps like the tarpon, but a flat-out dash of 100 yards or more that requires good nerves and better tackle.

Hunting the permit—so tough a flat-sided fighter I think of it as a scrappy bluegill grown to monster proportions—and channel bass is carried out much like bonefish stalking. But the permit is not an overly common fish and is usually spotted while bonefishing. It's a great trophy and many Keys anglers spend years before getting lucky enough to land one.

The channel bass, or redfish, is another bottom feeder and at certain times of year can be stalked and hunted like the bonefish. The runs aren't as spectacular but it's a game fighter nonetheless.

I should hasten to say that hunting fish isn't confined to the Florida Keys, although this area takes much of its fishing renown from the unusual opportunities for "hunting" that it affords.

To my knowledge there is no other place in the world of fishing where tarpon can be stalked as they are in the Keys during May, June and July each year as the migrating fish enter the back country of Florida Bay inside the Keys to feed before continuing their northward migration.

There's another great saltwater fighter—one of the rarest, most elusive and highly prized trophies in the world of sport fishing—that is "hunted" regularly. Far-ranging and solitary, he's held some anglers in thrall all of their lives without their ever bringing one to gaff. That's the broadbill swordfish.

Headquarters for one fleet of specialized boats and the breed of sharp-eyed skippers needed to hunt swordfish centers on Montauk, at the tip of Long Island. Here the broadbill angler can set out on a hunt for these big-eyed billfish.

Rising high above the deck of a sport-fisherman rigged for swordfish is the "broadbill tower," where the skipper can run the boat with a duplicate

Leaping, twisting, shaking when the hook first stings, tarpon are terrors.

set of controls while scanning the water for the big cruising fish. For the broadbill can regularly be seen basking on or just below the surface, usually alone. When this happens, the bait is run out and the boat begins maneuvering to present it in just the right way to attract the swordfish without spooking it.

The angler waits in the fighting chair braced for the strike—if it comes, which is discouragingly seldom. If it does, you've got to have the precise judgment to let the big fellow run just long enough to get the bait securely in its jaws before striking. When you think the fish is ready, you throw on the drag and really hit the broadbill with all your strength. Then hang on for the fight of your life!

Given the difficulties of first finding the fish, then getting it to strike and finally landing the brute, it's no wonder that only a few hundred broadbill swordfish have ever been caught on rod and reel. This has got to be rated the most glamorous of "hunted" fish.

But hunting fish isn't confined to salt water.

Using our fish-hunting definition—see the fish first, present the lure directly to it—gives us a few inland species that we can hunt successfully too. Most notably the Atlantic salmon.

Standing waist-deep in the rushing water of the Miramichi or Matane rivers in eastern Canada, the dry fly fisherman waits expectantly. He's watching for the flash that indicates a moving salmon. Once spotted, the fish is cast to and with luck hooked. More fish are taken with wet flies, but for sport and the "hunting" element, I believe the dry fly wins top honors. Personally, I prefer the dry fly for trout or salmon above any other kind of fishing.

Trout can be hunted with fly rod too, when they're rising to insects or nymphs. While the fish itself may not be seen, the feeding disturbance is apparent and so the element of "hunting" is certainly present.

How about hunting for bass? I would have doubted that this was possible until a trip to Lake Ouachita in Arkansas a few years back. It was my first visit to the lake and I wondered why my boat

33

Jack crevalle—of permit clan—is tackle tester.

school waiting for crippled shad to drift down to their depth are the real lunkers, not wanting to waste energy in a surface-feeding frenzy when they can grab an easy meal by just waiting below. The trick here is to get your lure down through the school of smaller fish without some youngster's grabbing it.

Pretty much the same conditions prevail for freshwater white bass, or the landlocked variety of striped bass that has been introduced to the Santee-Cooper impoundment of South Carolina and other large freshwater lakes. (Many biologists believe these two species belong to the same family.)

In either case the fisherman watches for the water commotion that indicates surface-feeding fish, or for the flock of gulls that gather over the feeding school to pick up scraps. The birds can be seen at long distance but the trick is to get in casting range before the stripers or white bass have left the area. The feeding schools move quickly and may surface again a mile from where last seen.

It's challenging and exciting work and you need a fast outboard motor to follow the schools. But once into fish you can catch them as fast as you can cast, in the case of white bass. The stripers take a little longer; 15 and 20 pounds is not an unusual size for the freshwater variety in Santee-Cooper.

In some of the big Texas lakes, once the school of white bass is located, a cast to the bottom with a heavy spoon or jig is the accepted fishing method. The lure is jigged off the bottom in good-sized jumps—and some good-sized fish are usually the result.

In all of the fishing I have mentioned, the element of *hunting* that's involved makes the sport just that much more interesting and challenging. The idea of pitting yourself against either a single fish or a school that you can actually see before trying to tempt them adds the seasoning that I've grown to love in this type of fishing.

I think the two most important things you should bring with you when hunting fish are: 1. a top-notch guide wise in the routes and feeding habits of the fish in his locality, and 2. a pair of sharp eyes, reinforced with a good pair of Polaroid sunglasses.

If you've never tried hunting for fish, you're missing an approach to the wonderful sport of angling that will test your nerves, your skill and your tackle. I'll be looking for you when the tarpon run next spring. Stand still—and keep your eyes peeled!

partner, a native of the area, brought us to a stop within sight of the big dam that creates the lake. We were well out in deep water and in a spot that looked barren and undistinguished to me except for a few flecks of foam on the calm surface. We just waited, and I kept my questions to myself.

Without warning, at least an acre of the surface suddenly exploded all around us as hundreds of largemouth bass crashed into a big school of shad minnows! We immediately threw small spoons into the melee and were rapidly rewarded with a two-pounder apiece.

Not exactly hunting? I think it comes close enough to fill the bill.

Interestingly enough, when the bass school after shad in Ouachita and other big lakes of the Mid-South, they are usually all of a size—maybe up to two or three pounds. But lurking under the

# CHAPTER 5

# WILD STRUGGLE
# TO CAPTURE A MOUNTAIN LION

We pulled the horses up and rested a moment, letting them blow. I sat there looking around me at the immense sweep of scenery here in the Green River country of east-central Utah. This was, I reflected, a country of unusual and anguished shapes. The trees were twisted. The wind-eroded mountains formed weird angles. Here and there on a flat plain, a red mesa thrust up in the middle of nothing. Boulders in jumbles were rounded by erosion. And elsewhere jagged shards of rock had broken from faults to plummet in scattered heaps.

If ever there was perfect, wild and lonely country for mountain lions to live in, this was it. When we had decided to try to do a mountain lion hunt as one of our OUTDOORSMAN TV series, we'd checked a number of states to see what each might offer. Utah appeared to be the best bet. And now, with the hunt in progress and lion country spreading for endless miles around us—without the slightest touch of civilization to spoil it—I was sure we had made the proper decision.

Jack Peters, my guide, motioned down below us and we started moving again. "There's a spring down there," he said. "I want to check it."

As we worked our way down I was sure that Jack would go right to the water to look for tracks. When, however, we had got down there and dismounted, he paid no attention but started around to where the snag of an old lightning-struck pine thrust up against the rocks. I was looking at all the deer tracks around the spring and thinking to myself that this would be a perfect spot for a lion to bushwhack a meal.

Jack called across and said, "This sure looks like cat to me." He was pointing to the base of the old pine snag.

I went to where he was, and there at the foot of the stump were dark, dried droppings with deer hair in them.

"Around a waterhole," Jack said, "they'll usually pick the same spot—just like a dog in town picks a certain tree. When a lion makes its feeding circle every week or so, it will check its tree or boulder, probably to see if any other lion has been around."

The sign looked old. However, Jack noted that it had not been rained on. And he remarked that it had rained and snowed hard up in this country five days ago.

"What do you think?" I asked.

"I think this cat should be back in three or four days. But I also think there may be a way to dope out about where it is right now."

To me, guides like Jack Peters are amazing people. Even in unfamiliar country, he'll soon figure out the most likely hunting circles the big cat will make. If he can cut down the time between when a cat was at a certain point, and the moment he gets his hounds on a hot trail, he is sure to up his chances of success. Mountain lions are found in such vast country that just casting about indiscriminately to locate a trail is all but useless.

For the first time on the hunt, I was now filled with excitement. I kept telling myself that it might be days before we caught up with this cat. And that there was a lot more possibility we'd never find it than that we would. But at least we had seen cat sign and now the really active part of the hunt was entered.

It seemed odd to me not to be carrying a rifle. We didn't intend to kill the lion if we got one treed. We were going to try to rope it and take it in alive.

As most readers probably know, my home state was South Dakota and I did a stint as Governor there a few years ago. When we decided to do a lion hunt for our TV show, I hit on the idea of presenting the lion alive—if we got one!—to the zoo at Custer State Park, in the Black Hills near Custer, South Dakota.

In fact, I had no great desire to kill a lion as a trophy. In the past the mountain lion has been bountied, trapped, shot by professional federal and state hunters until today it is actually one of our somewhat endangered species. Stockmen have been vociferous in their desire to have every lion killed. Many who've never had any difficulty whatever from mountain lions have been in the forefront of the battle to bring the great cats to total extinction.

Fortunately, within the last few years, conservation people have seen the light and have battled just as diligently to save the mountain lion. Today many states protect it entirely—except in specific instances, as when a single animal becomes a stock killer. Other states have the lion on the game list, and offer only certain seasons, just as with deer or elk or game birds, when it may be hunted. As long as huge blocks of wilderness are maintained, probably the lion today is in no real danger. And, as time goes on, it will unquestionably receive better and better protection everywhere.

The mountain lion, or as it has been variously called, puma, cougar, "panther," and "painter," is truly one of our most interesting species, and one of the most amazing cat species in the entire world. Thousands of years ago, this cat was able to adapt itself to almost every conceivable condition of climate and terrain. There were mountain lions in the Everglades and the other large swamp wildernesses of the Southeast. They existed in the eastern mountains, far up into portions of New England. Although there were certain areas in the interior U.S. where lions were probably not in residence, they were abundant from far down in Mexico, and even much farther south than that, and they prowled the mountains and deserts throughout the entire Rocky Mountain region. They were established on the Pacific slope and far up into British Columbia.

Today there are a few lions in the secluded places of the Deep South and Florida. They are gone from all of their ancestral eastern range. In Texas, where they were once plentiful especially in the south and west, there is today only a remnant. A few are taken each year in the brush country and deep in the Big Bend country. But in the unsettled, roughest portions of Arizona, Colorado, New Mexico, and Utah, as well as a few of the other mountain states, the handsome, secretive mountain lion still holds its own. In a few other places in the Northwest, such as Vancouver Island, it is still abundant.

A common habit and routine of all wild cats is that they stake out a domain and then patrol it, hunting. Usually the hunt travel is in a large roughly circular area. Because the lion is large, and thus requires a substantial amount of food, it must lay out a large region for its hunting. This means that on the average a lion will return, depending on how the hunting is, to the same general spots only once every week to 10 days. Such locations as waterholes, where all game must come, are favorites, and of course are sure to be visited.

A big male lion, or tom, is a loner. He stays with a female only during mating. If he happens to hang around until time for her to have her kits, she'll drive him off. Males of all the cats, even house cats, will kill young if they find them. The female brings meat to her den as soon as she has weaned her young, and soon they learn to eat it and to follow her and learn to hunt.

Quite often it is young lions that prey on livestock. One runs into a band of lambing sheep and has an orgy of blood letting, because it has just recently learned the art of killing. An old lion that has lost many of its teeth, or been crippled in one way or another (such as by porcupine quills in its mouth), also will resort to livestock killing occasionally. But in almost all of our lion country today, the mountain lion lives predominantly on deer. Deer are its natural and staple food and have been for centuries. An exception are the lions in javelina country of the Southwest and Mexico. Mountain lions eagerly kill javelina, and the little desert pigs appear to be a diet staple. Probably one reason is that the pigs are easy to catch.

The sensory abilities of the lion are legendary. They have extremely acute hearing and sight and a very fine nose. They have a fantastic ability for keeping out of sight. Many a trapper, or lion hunter who uses dogs, has never seen a lion except in a trap or in front of hounds, and yet he may have spent years in lion country and hung up a hundred lion hides.

When a lion makes a kill, it will eat what it wants, then drag the carcass to a secluded or cool place and cover it with sticks and leaves. Then the animal will lie up and rest until hungry again and go back to feed once more. If the weather is such that the meat does not become tainted, the lion will stay around and finish almost every bit of the kill. This is an interesting habit, and well illustrates that the mountain lion is not by nature an indiscriminate killer, or a "thrill" killer. However, it does not favor spoiled meat and will leave to make another kill if the weather is so warm the meat begins to smell.

There has been much controversy for years over the inroads lions may or may not make on deer herds. It is a rather ridiculous and academic argument at best. No doubt a lion kills the easiest animal it can get. This automatically would mean it will take old or crippled animals, those in poorest health. However, a hungry lion does not purposely look for an easy target, unless it simply stumbles upon one. But, since mountain lions do not exist in large numbers—this law of nature is true of all large predators because the larger the predator the more living and hunting room it needs—there is little to fret about so far as harm to the deer population. After all, we have in most areas more deer than we need. Each year there are two-deer, three-deer, four-deer areas for hunters.

When there were far more lions than there are now, there were still plenty of deer. So what the lions take makes really no difference whatever. Another item to remember it that in many lion ranges, almost no hunters operate. The terrain is too tough and remote. A single lion might cover an area of well over 100 square miles. If it took one deer a week it could scarcely make a dent in the natural increase. . . .

On the 10th day of November we left New York and wound up at Fruita, Colorado, where Jack Peters lives. Jack doesn't hunt in Colorado, because of the restrictions on lion hunting there. However, his home is only a short hop from the eastern border of Utah. He goes into his favorite country west of the Green River, a remote wilderness that I have already partially described.

Jack Peters is a real artist at his business. He knows the country in an uncanny manner. He knows the cats and seems to actually think like one. He also knows lion dogs, and has spent years establishing a strain of hounds best suited to his hunting style. Lion hunters have very biased— and diverse—opinions about what is or isn't a good dog. Many have used Airedales mixed in with a hound pack. Some have even employed fox terriers to help harass a lion at close quarters. Almost any dog that has a good nose and that will stay with a treed lion and bark continuously can handle these animals. Nonetheless, every professional lion guide wants exactly what *he* wants. The average lion hound is usually some cross among Trigg, Walker, Redbone, and even Bloodhound.

Jack Peters knows his hunting territory, clear from the southern border of Wyoming south to the "four corners" were Utah, Colorado, Arizona and New Mexico meet, as well as he knows his dogs. It's a mammoth country, with broad valleys and awesomely rough mountains. There is little grass, except along the rivers and around the waterholes. Here the deer and elk live on browse, and on what grass they can find.

Some of this country can be traveled by Jeep. Such travel keeps forcing game into the rougher portions. This suits the lions just fine. It suits Jack Peters, too. His home place is roughly 150 miles north of what I've called the "four corners." Yet I believe you could blindfold him and set him down anywhere in between and he'd instantly know where he was. The rougher it is, the better Jacks likes it.

We went into the edge of the hunting country and set up a camp. After that first night in camp we began to scout the area. We started out by Jeep and Jack said nothing about horses. The more we traveled, the more I wondered how we were going to get to the quarry and then get the camera and the sound equipment there, too. I never cease to be shaken by the difficulties involved. It takes a tremendous amount of planning, and it takes a great deal of savvy not only on the part of the guide but on the part of Halmi and Dichter, too. It also takes one heck of a big slice of pure and unadulterated luck.

When we had ridden so long I thought we ought to be almost to California, and kidded Jack about that, he suddenly pointed to a distant mesa-like ridge. Skylined there were a pair of saddle horses waiting for us. Starting hours before we did, one of Jack's men—Ernie—had ridden out here to meet us at this prearranged spot. Now Jack and I were to swap the Jeep for the horses, ride into country too rough for the Jeep to travel. Then after a long circle farther down the valley we'd reswap.

We left the Jeep and rode over the ridge. Jack kept his eyes searching every moment now for lion sign. He told me that you seldom stumble on anything worthwhile, unless you find sign at a waterhole or happen to find a kill a lion has made. In some of the smaller ravines there was snow. Jack kept checking each of these, but found nothing. Presently, as I have described in the beginning, he took me to the spring and found the lion droppings.

As we left the spot, he said, "Anyway, we know a lion is in this country, and it is within a few days' hunting of us right now. A lion hunter has to do a lot of guessing, but I always figure if I come out right half of the time that's better than hunting blind and without clues."

We rode on, checking what little snow there was, and really combing the country around each waterhole. It was beginning to get dusk when we dropped over a ridge and down to the valley to trade back to the Jeep again.

That evening during supper Jack was thoughtful. Finally he said, "I think we'll hunt tomorrow through the country south and west of where we saw that sign. I have a hunch about where that cat is, and I believe we might as well play it just as if I was right—whether I am or not."

He explained that he had to guess at the age of the droppings, but he was sticking to three or four days. The cat he guessed would take a week to nine or 10 days to make its hunting circle. And now as he went on I realized what an amazing amount of hunting craft he had.

"A lion," he said, "will work his circle the same way each time, almost track for track, IF the weather is such that he can always be hunting into the wind. If the wind switches, he'll cut across and work the circle backwards. We've been having wind steadily from the north. That means he went north and west. Right about now he has got to be coming south, so he can swing around and get the wind again."

There was the problem of how best to handle things to get Halmi and Dichter to the right place at the right time. It was going to be tricky. But we planned as best we could. Jack and I would hunt on horseback. The others would come by Jeep. Jack knew the country perfectly and he said now:

"Actually this is a lucky layout. If the cat is about where I think it should be, we'll be in a valley and they'll be on a ridge where they can hear the hounds. Of course, if the lion is jumped and runs the wrong way, we can't be sure Bob and Mark can get to us in time. All we can do is try. I think it's best for just the two of us to go on horses, however. The party will be far too unwieldy otherwise."

I was not at all worried about Halmi knowing what to do. If he was within hearing distance of hounds, you could bet he'd be on the job and with camera running. Bob has had tremendous, worldwide experience and he has an uncanny sense of what to do and when to do it. Dichter would be with him. We could now only trust to luck—and hope Jack Peters' hunch had been right.

The weather up until now had been bad. There had been some rain, and then as a cold front had passed through snow flurries had followed. But when we turned in that night the clouds were shredding and above them we could see the star-studded sky.

We tumbled out next morning while it was barely getting light. Jack had already sent two horses ahead, and a Jeep with his hounds in it. After breakfast he and I climbed into one Jeep and Bob and Mark piled their gear into another. It was a mystery to me how we would ever meet. The night before, Jack and his helpers had talked about: "Where that wash comes down and there's a bunch of junipers." Or: "You remember the time we treed that big tom near the cut in the ridge where you go down into Green River? Well about a mile further up the ridge there's a bunch of cedar. Wait for an hour right near them." Few people realize how well guides get to know a certain country. It might have taken five years of steady hunting to be able to pinpoint places the way these people did.

After a 20-minute drive we came to the horses and the pickup-Jeep that had the hounds in it. As soon as they could hear Jack Peters' voice there was a chorus of impatient whines.

Jack smiled. "I sure like to hear 'em sounding keen."

We clambered on our horses and Ernie let the door open, freeing the hounds. They tumbled out and immediately started off. Jack called them to him and made them follow his horse. "Doesn't help to have a pack run you," he said. "You have to have good control—especially if you fellows are going to get any film."

As we rode northwest, Jack pointed each hound out to me. He had eight. Four were older, experienced ones and four apparently were first-season hounds. We had gone possibly half a mile when a doe bounded out of some brush and ran across the trail. Two of the younger hounds yelped and started after her. Jack let out a whoop. They stopped.

"How do you break them of running deer?" I asked.

"Well, that's a good question. We're lucky here because we have lots of deer. In places where they're scarce, it's a problem. But we never breed to incorrigible deer chasers. And sometimes we couple—that is, collar together—a young hound and a veteran and let 'em crisscross tracks until the younger one realizes deer aren't the thing we're after. The best way of all is to have a tame deer when you have half-grown pups. I had an old doe that I'd found crippled. I patched her up. She was a real expert at setting a pup straight. She'd pop 'em with her front feet and it didn't take the pups long to learn to stay away from her."

We'd gone possibly two miles when we came to some rougher country that followed the lower elevation of a ridge. It looked as though, years ago, boulders had been rolled off the higher land. Between them grew patches of stunted cedar and juniper. Below us there was a creek bottom. There were pools in places and in others merely a trickle. Willows and other brush grew profusely in spots and there was some grass near the water. Old deer sign was everywhere. From what Jack Peters had been telling me, I knew that since the start of the elk season many deer had moved to higher ground.

"I'm guessing that about three or four miles up here, we might run across that cat's track," Jack said. "If we weren't hampered by the movie-makin' equipment, we'd check the next valley over. But if we did hit a track over there, they'd never hear us, let alone catch up."

We wound around rocks, following game trails, and then we came to a clearer stretch. Jack hollered to his hounds. "Go on guys, find me one!"

Immediately the eight hounds fanned out. Some dropped lower down the sidehill. The others disappeared in the rough ledges above us. One old black-and-tan hound had his ears shredded and a bad scar running down his left ribs. He came back and looked at Jack. Jack laughed.

He said, "O.K., Drum, you can cheat if you have a mind to."

Then he explained to me, "Old Drum's as good a cold tracker as I've ever followed. But he'll wait till another hound opens up, and then he'll drift on over. If the scent's strong enough for them to handle, he'll tag along. But as soon as they start checking, and can't work it out, he'll get on it as

if to say 'stand back, the Old Man will handle it!"

We eased on up the valley for an hour. Nothing happened. We came to a miniature gorge where at one time a slide or dammed-up water had thrown big boulders together in heaps. One of the younger hounds suddenly gave tongue. Old Drum stopped and listened. Jack reined in his horse and pointed. The hound gave another long bay. Another hound joined in. One of the younger ones, below us, bolted right through our horses, heading for the others above.

Where we were there was no wind. Although the pack must have been 300 hundred yards above us, their voices filled the valley and even their excited, muted whines drifted clearly down to us.

I was suddenly all but overwhelmed by excitement. There is no sound on earth quite as wild and thrilling as hound voices saying they have struck a scent and are on their way. So much of hunting is caught up in the senses of the hunter . . . the sights, the sounds, the smells. Sitting tensely astride my horse now, wanting so desperately for this to be a true strike, feeling my heart pound and the warm sun touching me and hearing the drama of hound voices in this big, wild country, I knew this moment would never be forgotten. Then their cry swelled—and ended abruptly.

Jack said, "They must have hit his track where he climbed up after coming down here for water. They probably can't follow it on the dry going. But if they can just cold trail him to where he's bedded, we just might make up several hours on him and get him roped. Let's stay put right here until they straighten it out."

I caught myself saying aloud, "Stay with it, don't lose it," every time a hound spoke now. Then one gave tongue farther away, and the others it was evident ran over and joined. The volume swelled. I felt as is something was barely brushing the hairs on the back of my neck. It soon became obvious that the lion had followed the gorge upward.

Jack said, "Just right, we can rendezvous with the camera crew in fine shape if he'll just stay on the rim country. Down here it'd be a mess."

Now we started following the climbing hounds. It was rough going. They kept losing the scent and we'd stop, listening intently, trying to catch the slightest sound above the heavy breathing of our horses. I reflected that man must have some very basic instincts about stalking and tracking, and following hounds. This suddenly seemed the most important thing I had ever done. Why a hunter throws himself into such an endeavor as if his very life depended on the outcome, I'll never fully understand.

After the hounds had lost the tracks four or five times, I recognized one particularly deep bay. It always seemed to be the one to open the next chorus. "Who is that?" I asked.

"Old Drum, he's showing 'em how it's done," Jack answered. "I hope you can get close enough to see him work. He'll always follow places where a cat would logically travel. You'd think he'd lived with them. A few of his pups are going to be just as good."

Little by little we made the top. Jack rode on top of some high ground and then I saw him wave. He came back and said: "We're in luck. The others must have heard 'em. I see the dust of the Jeep."

On the level ground we could now keep up with the hounds. It was the highest drama to watch them work. When they'd lose the scent, they'd fan out and steady down, like so many detectives.

Soon the Jeep caught up to us. Jack and Ernie had a hurried confab, planning where Ernie could hold the Jeep and still be able to get close if the hounds hit it off on a hotter scent. It began to sound as though the dogs had run into increasing trouble. Then suddenly several of them broke into a steady cry.

Jack yelled, "They've jumped him!"

As we listened, we tried to control our excitement and piece together what had occurred. The cat must have been bedded down in a bunch of high rocks when he'd first heard hounds. Then, when the Jeep hurried ahead, it seems possible that noise confused the cat. Not knowing which way was safe, he'd hesitated.

The delay had been most fortunate, had given us a much needed advantage. For even now, on the dry going, the scent was far from perfect. When the trail turned sharply on ground unprotected from the wind, most of the hounds overran, some of them roaring ahead at least 50 yards before circling in confusion. Again, each time, old Drum straightened out the puzzle.

I thought in desperation, "The blasted cat is going to give us the slip yet—and here we are so near." I wondered how Halmi would ever know where to go. And then with astonishment I suddenly saw Bob way up ahead, with his camera. He was waving frantically. As we raced ahead I could see the grin on his face. I knew at once that he had got film of the cat on the run. What a guy!

Luck stayed with us. The cat didn't drop back into the valley. Now the hounds could hang onto the trail better. Their cry reached wonderful crescendoes when scent was good, then diminished when they had difficulty. But it never stopped

completely now. I was riding behind Jack and suddenly I saw the cat lope across some high ground about a quarter of a mile ahead. Again Halmi was in a good spot, on the same ridge. We were astonished that the cat had not spotted him and turned. We paused atop the ridge where I'd seen the lion, and we listened intently. The hounds were still running strong. Then abruptly their cry changed. It came from one place. There were several long bellows, followed by a wild symphony of staccato yelps.

"They've treed him!" Jack shouted. "Come on!"

The rest was anticlimax. To be sure, it was exciting to ride up and see the lion, a fine three-year-old male, in the upper branches of a tree. It was completely absorbed with watching the hounds. Occasionally it would hiss and snarl. Some of the hounds seemed half cat. They'd get a good ways up the tree before falling back. But now the real thrills were over. The chase was the thing. I wished it might have gone on and on.

Jack is a past master at handling lions. He smoothly slipped a noose of piano wire around the tom's neck. He used a long pole but still had to get in the tree with the cat. I snubbed the end of the wire around a tree and then we caught up the hounds. When we pulled the cat out I had a moment of apprehension because where I was standing and holding the wire, seemed just too darned close for comfort.

When the cat hit the ground I swiftly hauled in slack. The lion's breathing was hardly restricted before Jack had him trussed up like a bundle and we were able to loosen the noose around his neck. Jack now gagged him with a stick in his mouth.

What a handsome specimen he was. We guessed him at about 115 pounds. His coat was slick and clean. We slung him up on Jack's saddle horse— and believe me a horse has to be well trained to stand for that!—and we packed him out of the rough country to where the Jeep was parked.

Bob Halmi and Mark Dichter were elated. I'd been a bit busy to ask just what they had accomplished, but they had got both the film and sound we wanted. Luck we'd had, that was certain. But we'd had tremendously good management, too, by Jack Peters and his crew. As we rode toward camp I looked at the great, rugged mountains on the skyline, wondering how many cats were left. The mountain lion is certainly one of North America's most exciting game animals, and it's good to know that game departments are helping its survival.

**Halmi saw lion before the hunters.**

Eager hounds leap up into tree trying to reach mountain lion. Opposite top, Joe stays well away from lassoed cat. Bottom, subdued and tied, lion is packed out of Utah canyon for shipment to zoo.

King salmon Joe Foss caught in

British Columbia was strong and

full of fight. Joe and fishing buddy Bob Munger

find it makes delicious eating as well.

Bob Munger, Joe Foss and guide
Bill Love cross Stevens Lake,
British Columbia, at dawn.

Guides Bob Lee and Bob Lee, Jr.,
took Joe on long, exciting stalk to get this
Rocky Mountain goat in British Columbia.

# CHAPTER 6

# STRANGE BEAR HUNT
# IN BRITISH COLUMBIA

I really can't remember when it was that I first wanted to go to British Columbia. Seems as if I always had. I do recall that during World War II one of the favorite topics during bull sessions was hunting and fishing. A tepid night in the Pacific made some guys truly worth recording, they'd get so wound up and flowery describing their favorite spots. And, those who had been to British Columbia could run up a performance second to none.

I presume everyone who loves the outdoors has at one time or another tried to picture how a certain area was years ago, before civilization had changed it and its game populations. Many a time I've thought, when looking at a sweep of mountains maybe with roads going across them: "What I'd give to have been the first human here." At any rate, I knew that parts of Canada were at least far less disturbed by civilization than much of the U.S. I gathered that most of British Columbia might be compared to what our own Northwest was like perhaps half a century ago. And so, when we decided to make one of the films for our OUT-DOORSMAN series in British Columbia, I was really eager to get going.

Now then, taking a hunting trip to see the country and collect a trophy is a whole lot different from making the same trip to shoot film and tape the actual sounds of the same hunt. One of the most difficult parts is that with few exceptions game is most active early in the morning and late in the afternoon. This presents often truly insurmountable light problems for the camera, and at best serious difficulties.

Next, getting a hunter to a spot where he can collect a trophy is easy compared to putting a film crew and equipment there. A hunter and his guide can stalk and sneak and crawl to a position for a long-range shot without much trouble. But when you think of the problems of lugging camera and sound equipment, of getting set up where the range will be short enough for the camera to work effectively, having the hunter and game so positioned that the light is right, getting your people and equipment hidden. . . well, it might be compared to running the 100-yard dash bundled in a space suit with an anvil in each hand.

Even before we left New York, I was rather appalled at the amount of equipment we were going to have to operate with. When Bob Halmi, the show's co-producer and cameraman, and Dick Lyford, the sound man on this trip, and I were ready to load onto the plane, the only thing I could think of was a Hollywood set in the midst of some epic.

I told Bob, "If getting this stuff on location is as hard as getting it on the plane, we better call it off right here."

We flew to Toronto, westward across Canada to

Vancouver, and finally to Smithers, British Columbia. We'd previously booked a bush pilot to fly us from here on up north another hundred miles to Stevens Lake, where our guide, Bill Love, had a camp. We hadn't figured quite what a tussle there might be this time of year, up in the north country, with ground fog. But we soon found out.

When we loaded up next morning at Smithers for the run north, however, things looked all right. Mist was rising from the water and the pilot felt this was a good sign. We should have no trouble. What I kept wondering as we loaded was how we'd ever cram all that equipment into the small float plane. However, we had it done at last and were off. We'd not gone 40 miles when the stuff below us thickened. It became such a solid deck that we knew we'd have to get beneath it.

The pilot worked the plane down, and got into a valley between high mountains. The game we immediately began seeing took our minds off the narrow spots the plane was moving through. We counted 65 mountain goats on peaks on either side of the plane. In some places we were so close we could see horns, and easily distinguish adults from kids. It was indeed a rough country, and I was thrilled by seeing it as I had visualized it many times.

But it was different from much of the Rockies that I knew more intimately. Timberline was not as clearly defined. Slides had cleaned some slopes entirely. On others, spears of scrub and brush ran up like arrowheads. But it was beautiful. Pockets of snow with their resultant temperature influence in the immediate vicinity caused wisps of clouds to cling here and there.

At last our pilot thought we must be over Stevens Lake. But now the stuff below was so thick we couldn't get down. He circled, planning what might be best to do. Finally he decided to try for another lake he knew of, a smaller one, nearby. Soon he found it. Conditions were better here, and presently he put us down.

There was nothing for us to do now but wait around until the sun had dissipated the ground fog enough so we could move back to Stevens. So, to kill time, I got out my Shakespeare spinning rod, tied on a red-and-white spoon and began casting to see what might be here. On the very first try a rainbow of about two pounds came darting along, following the lure. It was about to hit when it saw the shadow of the plane. It did a quick 180-degree turn, swam lazily away. On almost every cast I had a similar trout follow. I kept thinking what a sportsman's paradise all of this vast country must be. Here I had just cast out into the lake, not trying the

outlet, which is usually where fish feed the most in lakes like this, and here I was pulling trout to the lure cast after cast!

After an hour of this, we decided we could now probably make it back to Stevens Lake. I dismantled the rod. The pilot said to me, "Joe, would you like to take her over the ridge to Stevens?"

I got into the pilot's seat and in a few minutes we were over Stevens. There were several good clear patches in the fog. I got a look at Bill Love's camp nestled invitingly on shore, and I swung around and landed as close as I could. My thought was that in such country as this there could well be grizzlies not far from camp. If that was so, I did not want to disturb them more than necessary. The area had been well described to us when we made our reservations. Stevens Creek, and the Kispiox River, were here. The bears should at this time be feeding on spawning salmon in these streams. We hoped to photograph and shoot a trophy boar bear—as big old males are called— and it would be a shame if I ran off our quarry getting us to camp.

I taxied to shore and Bill Love was already there to meet us. He had an old horse, named Derby, hitched to what we called a "stone boat" when I was a kid. Probably many readers have never seen this crude contraption, but every farm kid did when I was one. It is a simple drag made with a couple of rough-hewn logs for runners, and with cross pieces for a bed. The front ends of the logs are cut off on an upward slant so they don't catch in the ground. A horse is hitched with lines to this primitive bare-ground sleigh. Simple but efficient. We piled our duffle in a big heap on this "stone boat" and started off for camp with Derby skidding the load along.

Most guides in British Columbia like to have a permanent camp. There are numerous old sites that were used by trappers. Often such a place is located at the confluence of several waterways on which the trapper has run lines upstream to the various headwaters. Such a valley setup with mountains lifting on all sides is perfect for game. A camp located in such a spot allows a hunter to walk several miles in any direction from camp and usually find several species of game. Of course, there are scores of other places that a pack string of horses can get to. But a camp as described gives the guide or outfitter a bit more peace of mind. In late fall he doesn't have to fret, as the fellow with a string of horses does, about getting snowed in.

There were two hunters already at Bill Love's camp, and they turned out to be fine gents. They were from Charlotte, Michigan—Harvey Holcomb and Bob Munger. Harvey is a farmer. Bob has a sporting goods store and is an archery enthusiast. I knew that several archers had shot a number of grizzlies. But something about the combination of Munger and his bow, plus a grizzly, right there with us, upended my hair.

We all shook hands and talked a bit about the flight up, discussed the spawning salmon, and I asked questions about the bears. Funny thing about hunters. In the space of 20 minutes of visiting, we were friends. I have long thought that the easy rapport among men who have a common interest in fish and game makes the sports of fishing and hunting really something special. People who do not pursue these pastimes can hardly understand. It's difficult to explain. But I know one thing, it's far different from the feeling, for instance, among a group of golf buffs. It's a lot more solid, a deeper understanding.

As most readers know, Bob Halmi has taken game pictures all over the world. He's Hungarian and is a fiery sort of gent, always all business. Bob was impatient. He wanted to get going immediately. He felt we should find as quickly as possible some sites where the bears were feeding and where we might be able to get some of the footage we wanted. But Bill Love discouraged us just a bit. The bears, he explained, half in apology as if somehow it was his fault, weren't working the creeks after salmon as hard as they did most seasons. There was a terrific crop of blueberries up in the hills. The sweetness of those berries was pulling the bears like a magnet.

"That," Bob muttered, "would be our luck! Bears scattered all over the mountains."

That day we hunted hard for possible sites for our setup. But we came in toward evening with nothing accomplished. We'd have to spend the next day scouting, too. Bob was uneasy. I should explain that when we make films of this sort, obviously time is limited. Every day must count, because much of the time we are already scheduled ahead to do another film elsewhere. The pressure is tough on all concerned, and hold-ups in weather and because of game situations are most exasperating, yet a permanent, built-in part of this profession. It is not the carefree life many viewers imagine.

At least we had a comfortable camp. I had visualized accommodations that would probably be pretty rough, way back in wild country such as this. But first of all Bill Love's wife was there to do the cooking and she did a wonderful job. We had a warm, dry, well-ventilated place to roll out our rubber mattresses and bed rolls.

After another day of scouting, during which we found several locations that we thought just might produce, we felt better, and ready to go. We had selected a place for me where I would be in a tree. This spot was near the shore. There was some bear sign, but it was really not to fresh. I was in place before dawn.

There is no time of day quite as thrilling as those moments when the day is pushing back the night. Over the peaks a pale bronze seemed to roll up the deep purple. Birds and small squirrels chattered. They seemed, I thought, to have very special, quizzical sounds for use at dawn. I could look down upon and into the water. There was a constant movement made by spawning salmon.

I was enjoying the coming of the day. But as time passed and no bear showed up, I was a bit uneasy. At last I was about to climb down and give it up when I heard the rapid whistle of wings. It was an unmistakable sound—ducks. Six hooded mergansers swished into the water and swam directly toward me. The hooded merganser is a dashingly handsome little creature, colorful and quick. And now these began the most amazing display.

As the salmon released their eggs, fingerling rainbow trout were zipping around them, gobbling up the spawn. The mergansers, whose diet as many hunters know is heavily fish, were chasing the small trout and in turn gobbling *them* up. I became utterly fascinated by this panorama of the chain of life being enacted there before me. I could see a fat female salmon in the act of dropping her eggs. Near her lay a male, flapping his broad tail to spread the milt exuding from his body evenly over and around the eggs.

I could not quite see the small trout. But it was obvious the disturbance made by the salmon was attracting them in swarms. And then here came a merganser, moving with amazing speed. It darted in, dived, came up with a fingerling trout. Instantly the other five mergansers started chasing the one with the fish, trying to head it off this way and that, attempting to grab its fish. And meanwhile the fleeing feathered fisherman was desperately trying to get the trout turned so that it could gulp it down head-first. There was a partially submerged log below me that ran up into the stream. It was about six inches above water. Yet the agile, darting ducks just seemed to flow over the top of it in their chase.

I'd often heard how rough on fish mergansers are. I was now willing to believe it, although I presume the merganser population is not large enough to have any really serious effect on fish populations. After all, the waters where we were had both fish and fish ducks, and certainly the trout and salmon were not in short supply. Regardless, the show they were putting on was dramatic and exciting. I looked at my watch and at the light. It was 10 o'clock and light was beautiful. It had occurred to me that maybe Bob would want to film this salmon-trout-duck show if they'd just do it again next day. As it turned out, Bob was eager, and the next day at the same time he took 15 minutes of film that is one of the most interesting sequences showing the struggle for survival that I have ever seen.

But, good sequence or not, we still had not seen a bear. And now bad weather dropped in on us. It was too foggy and foul to try filming. To put in tour time, we broke out the Shakespeare spin tackle and went after the salmon. We filed down the barbs on the lures, and caught both coho—silver salmon—and kings, the big chinooks. We also took some very large Dolly Varden trout.

As we fished, however, we never for a moment took our minds off bears. We slung our rifles over our shoulders when we waded out any distance from shore. There have been cases of grizzlies somehow mistaking the noise and outline of a fisherman for something to tangle with. It is puzzling why they should do this. But grizzlies are very unpredictable.

It is possible that with so-so eyesight they may in dim light think at first that a fisherman is another bear. We'd been told of instances when a bear had wallowed halfway to a wading angler, then when the strange scent hit it, had wheeled and raced off in panic. But we couldn't be certain this panic bit would happen. If a sow with cubs happened to come after fish, and a cub squealed, the sow might blow up in rage and come for us.

The fishing was great. We could catch salmon one after the other. As most anglers know, the silver, or coho, is on the average not large. It averages five to 10 pounds. But it is a fine leaper and a violent battler. We had great sport with them. We also hooked numerous big kings. These were big, fresh-run fish, very strong and full of fight. Try that sometime on a light spinning rod and with a Remington grizzly rifle slung over your shoulder and you'll gather what sort of wild confusion we had!

Although we'd been enjoying ourselves, by now both Bob Halmi and I were very much concerned about getting bear footage. And what made it more exasperating, during the bad weather when we had no light for filming, several bears had been working Stevens Creek. We'd not seen them, but had found their telltale sign—half-eaten fish, rotten logs torn apart, rocks turned over where the animals had been seeking grubs in the damp earth.

We were overjoyed to get a weather change. The very first morning of good light we were all set up with the cameras and sound equipment. Again I was in a large tree. Although the early and late hours we knew would be most likely to produce action, our time here was now so short and critical that we determined to spend the entire day. It dragged on and on. We had to remain very still, of course, and the time seemed to plod along interminably. As the afternoon wore on, all of us I'm sure had built up discouragement to the point of debacle. By 5 o'clock the light had waned until it was marginal.

At last Bob and Dick came up to where I was. Dick said, "We've decided to give it up and go in. Bob feels we just don't have enough light from now on anyway."

I don't know what made me do it, but I suddenly was hit with the idea that since I'd put in this much time I might as well finish out the day. I said, "If you gents don't mind, I think I'll stay right through until dark."

Halmi muttered something in Hungarian. Then he said, "Be my guest." They turned and disappeared toward camp.

They had barely been gone 10 minutes when, within 20 feet of me, a huge grizzly appeared. I was simply overwhelmed and disbelieving. I was also filled with anguish and frustration that this should occur. I'd wanted to see a bear, that's sure—and yet to have it come with light down and Bob and Dick gone was the keenest sort of disappointment. The bear had moved in suddenly, and though I am sure it had not winded me, something was making it uneasy. I wondered if it had somehow caught the scent of Bob and Dick.

The bear charged into the clearing we'd selected as our shooting ground. Then it wheeled and charged away again. In a moment it came back. It reared up now on its hind legs. Somehow I was reminded by its actions of some big kid trying to imitate a gorilla. I was thinking what a fantastic sequence this would have been on film, and I could have wrung my hands in grief. I gave a low whistle to see what the bear would do. It settled down a bit, but then moved off. I heard a noise behind me and my hackles crawled. I turned slowly. It was Bill Love. I hadn't realized Bill had stayed.

The cold and the excitement had me shivering so that I could hardly speak. But I leaned down and whispered to Bill, "I saw the one we want!"

I was watching Bill's face, somehow thinking that he wouldn't believe me. And I was also thinking what a fool thing I'd said. The one we want!

We had the bear here and no camera or light! Bill didn't speak. We watched for five minutes. Then I heard Bill suck in his breath. The bear had come back. I had often heard that bears are extremely individual, that once you see one, see how it acts, you can spot the same animal again, even year after year, and know it is the same one. Sure enough, this brute repeated motion for motion everything that it had done a few minutes before.

As the big bum went on and on he was really adding fuel to my complete frustration. He stood up, swayed. Over and over. He was a stunning specimen. His coat was in beautiful shape, the guard hairs so long that he seemed to swell up when he moved. His antics were punctuated by occasional low rumbles. Then the show was over as swiftly as it had begun. For no apparent reason the bear suddenly shot off out of the clearing, bending saplings that got in the way as if they were buggy whips. Bill and I stayed a few moments, breathless, then started silently back to camp. But we each knew, I'm sure, what the other was thinking. Why couldn't that confounded bear have done his act a half hour sooner!

That night, lying in my sack, I couldn't get the bear out of my mind. I knew Halmi, to whom of course we had excitedly related our experience, must be having the same difficulty. Someday, I thought, I'd like to make a film with no schedule, no crowding for time. But I suppose if that day ever comes something else will happen to foul up the plan. Making films is like that—a constant battle with animals, elements, cameras. If it isn't one, it's all three. We had made arrangements farther north to photograph goats, moose, caribou. We had exactly 24 more hours here at Stevens Lake.

The next day we went at it again, determined as ever. Our luck just had to change. We got set up and we waited, hour on hour. The sun became fairly warm. Insects droned. Occasionally a pine squirrel chattered. Salmon splashed in the shallows. Otherwise, there was only the vast silence of this huge wilderness. I kept listening for the crackle of sticks or the swish of saplings. I kept trying to conjure up a bear and to wish it here so hard that surely I could make the wish come true. But the day simply dragged along. At last the light faded.

Halmi came up and whispered, "That's that." He turned in dejection and left and Dick went with him.

Sometimes now, remembering, I wish I had gone in with Bob and Dick. I imagine Bill Love often thinks about that, too. But Bill came up near me and we stayed, curious, I guess, to see just how

frustrating a bear—or luck—might be. I glanced at my watch. I settled myself down and tried to relax. Nothing was going to happen, I kept telling myself. I should have gone in. Then suddenly, out there in the clearing, as if by magic a big boar grizzly appeared. I stared. Then I remembered to check my watch again. Bob and Dick had been gone exactly seven minutes!

It was not the same bear. But it was just as huge as the previous night's comedian. Bill Love whispered, "In a hundred years you couldn't see two such big grizzlies in two days!"

Very carefully I got down from the tree. The wind was perfect. The bear suspected nothing. I raised my Remington Model 700 and looked through the scope. There was still enough light to see the bear's skull, and its eyes. The range was a mere 20 yards! During these exciting minutes I did some thinking about the sport of hunting. I thought about how much difference one hour's time would have made for us. Sometimes only a few minutes can make the difference. In fact, it is the unpredictability of an animal like a grizzly that makes hunting the great sport that it is. The frustration that I felt was only part of the game.

There was something truly magnificent about this enormous brute. Even in the swiftly fading light its poise and movements had an amazing, unforgettable grace and ease. What a disappointment it was not to get one of these animals on film, and to get the kill we wanted! But I must admit that in that moment I was thrilled to have experienced these two evenings and their dramas. I lowered the rifle without firing a shot, beckoned to Bill Love, and quietly we stole away toward camp.

As viewers of this particular show will discover, not shooting a bear wasn't the end of the hunt. One morning we spotted a band of mountain goats on a high slope and we made a very exciting stalk to within close range of them.

Let me tell you, creeping up on a spooky critter like a watchful old billy takes some doing. But we were lucky and I finally bowled over a good one.

I have his mounted head on the wall of my den and looking at the trophy brings back fond memories of British Columbia. But the part of that hunt I enjoy most, I believe, is recalling how those two big bears looked. You don't have to shoot everything you see on a hunt like this for it to be a success and this was certainly true of those grizzlies.

I can see them still, as plainly as if it were yesterday. And someday I'll have the pleasure of hunting for one of these big bruisers again.

# CHAPTER 7

# THE NONSENSE PEOPLE BELIEVE ABOUT GUNS
## By Jack Mitchell

Ever since our hairy hunting ancestors squatted around a fire at the mouth of a cave and argued about the right shape for a flint spearhead, there has been constant controversy about this business of "ballistics" which Webster defines as "the science of the motion of projectiles in flight."

During my years in the gun and ammunition business, I've sat in on many a "hot-stove" forum and listened to all kinds of "experts" really warm up on the subject. The first of these sessions that I clearly remember was when I was a young hunter in a northern Wisconsin deer camp. Old Frank Bell, the best guide and shot in that jack-pine country, was holding forth on the unusual performance of an old black-powder rifle he once owned.

"You young squirts may not believe this, but that old .45-90 would shoot straight and flat for a mile and a half and then raise just a little."

One of us young city hunters backed up by one year of high school physics asked, "Mr. Bell, I kind of thought all bullets were affected by gravity and began to drop as soon as they left the muzzle."

Frank took a few puffs on his pipe and then calmly answered, "Not with this one, son. You see, the velocity of that bullet was so fast that gravity never even got a chance to work on it."

But the doubter persisted and bravely asked again, "But what made that bullet raise up like you said?"

Frank then settled everything by his statement, "That bullet was evidently just climbing up to its midrange trajectory."

There was a stunned silence at this amazing display of "expert" ballistic knowledge and Frank closed the meeting with, "Let's climb into those bunks now. Tomorrow we'll be hunting the Rose Lake burn and I'll be rolling you boys out before it's daylight in the swamp."

Frank was obviously a better hunter than a ballistician but even today I still keep running into shooters who actually believe that a rifle bullet rises above the line of the rifle bore, or line of departure. I think it's because the standard diagram of the rifle's line of sight, line of bullet departure, trajectory course, and points X, Y and Z, just plain confuses everyone.

Far be it from me to try and sound like another ballistics expert, but take a look at diagram C.

We've tried to simplify the usual complicated diagram and show you just three lines—(1) the *line of sight* lined up with your eye (2) the *line of departure* lined up with the bore of your barrel and (3) the downward-curving *path of the bullet*. In order to hit the target at C your sights are obviously lined up with C but your barrel is aiming at B a point above C in order to allow the downward path of the bullet to connect with C and score a hit. In order to do this, the bullet rises above the line of sight but it never rises above the line of the bore or the line of departure. The bullet just can't do this—it's against the law. Of gravity, that is.

Here's another question to try out in the "hot-stove" shotgun sessions. "Does a long shotgun barrel shoot farther than a shorter barrel?" This question has led to some dandy arguments—almost as hot as that stove you're sitting around.

I remember one day when I was a kid hunting ducks on a pass between two lakes in South Dakota. The prairie wind was strong in our faces and the bluebills, redheads and canvasbacks were coming over fast and high. We'd been watching a tall, lanky shooter in the blind next to ours unfold up to his full 6 feet 8 inches, stick up what looked like a "window-pole"—that gun barrel must have been at least 36 inches long—and nail those high flyers with amazing regularity.

"No wonder he hits 'em," I complained to my Dad. "He's halfway there when he stands up and that long barrel shoots higher, too." My Dad, who was a professional trapshooter for Remington as well as a great wing shot, only laughed . . . and then proceeded to demonstrate that his Remington automatic with a regular 30-inch barrel could reach up just as well, and produced a double out of the next bunch of high ducks.

That night in camp, Dad explained to me that the advantage of any barrel longer than about 26 inches is largely in the shooter's mind—*except* where he prefers a longer sighting radius for more precise pointing. It's easier to carefully point a yardstick than it is to point a one-foot ruler. However, the increase in velocity due to increased barrel length beyond this point is only slight and after 30 inches the extra barrel length is mainly for decoration and perhaps an added sense of personal power. Maybe the extra-long-barrel shooter likes to be a few inches closer to his game.

Dad also pointed out that the "long-tom" barrel was popular in the days of black-powder shotgun shells because this old-fashioned powder burned slower and took a longer barrel to hold the charge until the powder was completely burned. But don't you believe it when someone in that "hot-stove" league tells you, "My 36-inch barrel will outshoot your 30-inch barrel any day in the week and I can prove it."

And while we're on the subject of "hard shooting"—(and I hope you're still with me)—I'll bet you know some shooters who still believe that an autoloading or "automatic" rifle or shotgun doesn't shoot as "hard" as other types of guns because they believe that the force of the powder gases used to operate the action that extracts and ejects the fired

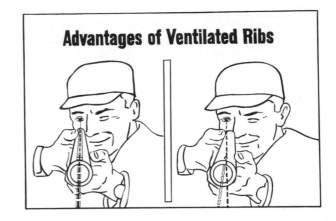

Diagram A: Broad, flat sighting plane of ventilated rib makes it easier for shotgunner to aim quickly and accurately, left, prevents cross-firing, right.

round and loads in a new round, is subtracted from the total force of gases and "weakens" or "lessens" the velocity of the bullet or shot charge.

In fact, the action of a modern autoloader stays in a locked position for full power until *after* the shot charge or bullet has left the muzzle on its way to the traget. So, again, you may now take your position around that stove and quietly wait for "weak autoloading actions" to enter the discussion and then strike a blow for truth and the reputation of American auto-loading guns. Thank you.

Speaking of shotguns, can you list the main advantages of a ventilated rib on a shotgun barrel? While this one isn't necessarily a ballistic question, there are some points on this that can probably stand discussion.

"*Overheated* barrel? I'm going back and find out where I can go to get hunting like that."

Actually, the heat-wave diffusion feature applies only to trap and skeet shooting where there is prolonged and rapid firing. One of the main advantages of a vent-rib barrel, and one too often overlooked, is faster barrel alignment because the flat top of the ventilated rib gives your eye a better and straighter sighting plane. If your eye is misaligned by as little as ½ inch at the stock this means a *4-foot* error in the point of impact at 40 yards. (See diagram A.)

I hope you plain-barrel shooters won't use this as an alibi when you miss your next shot but you can at least add this tip to your "technical qualifications" for the next meeting of your local hot-stove club.

When man took to war in the air and bullets were fired from aircraft, there were lots of ballistics questions raised. The professional ballisticians, of course, had the answers but the amateurs still had their doubts about the conclusions.

In World War II, I served as an aerial free-gunnery instructor in the U. S. Navy. Most of my time was spent in training candidates for gunners' wings on a machine-gun range. On rainy days, we went indoors for a chalk-talk on such technical subjects as bore-sighting turret guns and studying the apparent motion of attacking aircraft. In one of these stimulating sessions the yawns of my audience made a change in subject necessary so I put this ballistic puzzler on the blackboard:

"What happens to a bullet fired directly to the rear from an airplane traveling with the same velocity as the bullet?"

This woke up the class and some whispered discussions began to take place. Finally a smart young bluejacket disregarded military tradition and "volunteered" this answer:

"I think that if I had fired the bullet rearward from the plane—and could see it—it would appear to have the same velocity as on the ground."

When I asked, "Why?" He said, "Because I'd be moving away from it in the plane at the same speed—and it would look as though it had its normal velocity."

I questioned him further: "Since the forward speed of the plane and the rearward speed of the bullet are equal, wouldn't the bullet really stand still?"

No answer for a while—but everyone was painfully thinking. Then he said, "If I were standing on the ground, the velocity of the bullet would appear to be zero—canceled out—and it would drop vertically to the ground." (See diagram B.)

That did it—everybody got in the act and then an excited gunner burst out with, "Hell, if that was true you'd have to shake the bullet out of the barrel."

Fortunately for us all, the sun came out and I sent the class back to the range—still arguing and waving their arms.

After the War, I posed this question to our Chief Ballistics Engineer at Remington. He said,

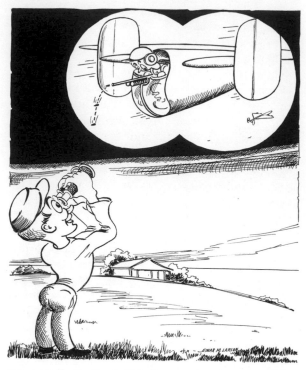

Diagram B: In the bullet-plane controversy, everything depends on your relative position. The ground observer would see the bullet falling straight down to earth.

"The boy was right. It is a matter of relative position. Motion must always be relative to some other object. So the gunner sees the bullet as moving because he's moving away from it—but to the ground observer the relative velocity is zero."

That's what the expert said and maybe all this can come in handy at the hot stove. Of course, it's purely theoretical but we want you to be fully prepared.

You're probably glad to see that I'm running out of space but if we ever meet again at a real hot-stove meeting, I'm the "expert" with the worried expression. You never know what will come up next.

Diagram C: The bullet never rises above the line of departure, but it does rise above the line of sight.

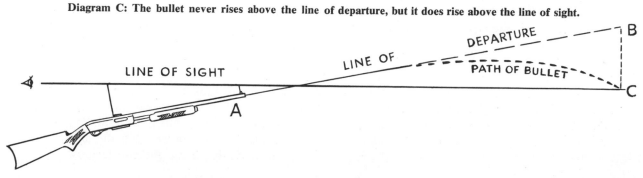

# CHAPTER 8

# THE SURPRISING WILDERNESS BEHIND FLORIDA'S SKYSCRAPERS

The Florida coastal swamp was a kind of puzzle that we were attempting to solve. Somewhere here in a maze of intricate waterways was hidden the huge alligator that we were going to try to take alive. There had been complaints about this 'gator. Probably the big reptile was harmless enough if left alone, but when a big one takes up residence in a place where fishermen or tourists or swimmers see it, they are afraid of it and they complain. The game department people in Florida get the complaint and it is up to them to move the nuisance alligator to a new home.

I was with Ron Davis, the Florida wildlife officer who was to do the job. We were easing along in his airboat. Bob Halmi was there with his camera gear, and Mark Dichter with his sound equipment. We were going to try to get on film and on sound tape for our show, THE OUTDOORSMAN, all the action that was sure to happen if and when we found the 'gator.

Presently Ron nudged the odd craft through a narrow opening and paused to look and listen. Then he got into the water, moved away and into tall grass. A few seconds later I was watching, appalled, as what looked like yard after yard of alligator came charging out and right toward the boat. Then Ron was running to leap aboard. He was handing me the gig and making sure his ropes were coiled and ready. His former instructions were

roiling through my mind:

"You'll get him gigged and hold on and I'll jump in with him. When I get his jaws clamped shut, we'll wrestle him aboard and. . . ."

At this point it suddenly occurred to me to wonder just what in the devil I was doing here anyway. There was no backing down now, but it was, I reflected, my own fault that I found myself in this preposterous predicament. Here I was, about to be a TV star in a slugging match with a bull alligator, and I wasn't so sure at that instant that I cared much about this variety of stardom—or martyrdom, either!

Over past years I've fished and hunted in Florida several times and I have always been greatly intrigued by what I found. When Bob Halmi and I became involved in doing our own TV series, I was eager to do at least one show in Florida. The most fascinating aspect of the state for our purposes was, it struck me, the fact that the cities of Florida had all been carved out of such a dense tangle of forest and swamp. The result was that within short distances even of many major cities there are still today vast blocks of some of the wildest country to be found anywhere in the United States.

Many of these are what can loosely be termed large stretches of swamp country. There is a most provocative fascination to me about this kind of terrain. There is a mystery about it. It seems almost to dare one to enter it, and to smirk as one leaves, as if knowing that never will all of its secrets be solved. There are drawbacks, to be sure. Much of this country is hot, and humid, and it swarms with a variety of annoying insects. Nonetheless, it gets under an outdoorsman's skin. It has an abundance of game. And, this Florida wilderness is not overrun, even in our teeming age. The state sells only a little over 2,000 nonresident hunting licenses annually, and hardly cracks 200,000 in resident licenses. That's not many hunters to spread over such a vast domain.

When I was connected with the American Football League and negotiations were underway for the Miami Dolphins to join the league, I listened to a great many stories about Florida's hunting and fishing. I went on some dove shoots I'll never forget. I saw as many deer come out of a swamp ahead of hounds—the legal and popular way of hunting in many parts of Florida—as I have seen anywhere during an open season. But when we got down to discussing a film to be made in Florida, I wanted to go further than just the hunting.

Why not, I thought, get acquainted with a warden who is right out in the field, hunt with him and use him in the show? Problems of conservation and game management have long intrigued me almost as much as hunting. I knew that Florida wardens have some very special problems, particularly in enforcement, because of terrain. There are, I had been told, a good many lawless types living off the beaten path—and off the country. I reasoned that the average hunter who'd be viewing this film must feel just like I did. Having a warden talk about enforcement problems concerning the game we were hunting or photographing would be most interesting.

To get us started, we contacted John Wilhelm. John works for the Florida Development Commission. His specific job is the sort that many a sportsman dreams of having. He takes in tow writers, and groups like ours, helps them locate what they need for stories and films, and tries to make sure that the results will be good exposure for Florida. John, we soon discovered, can come up with absolutely anything. Just name it and he knows where to find it.

"Where," I asked, "can we find a game warden to use in this film who is amiable, photogenic, knowledgeable and loquacious?"

John Wilhelm didn't even hesitate. "You're describing Ronnie Davis at Brooksville," he explained. "I'll contact him."

He did, and relayed word that Ron would be glad to help us, but there was one little hold-up. He'd had a complaint on a nuisance 'gator and he was going to have to catch it and move it to a new home.

"How could we get luckier!" I said enthusiastically. "There's a sequence that would be terrific for the show!"

We gathered via commercial airline at Tampa. There Halmi, Dichter and I piled our gear into the Heli-Porter. Wilhelm was to drive north, get Ron Davis, and meet us at the Crystal River airport. The 'gator job was near there, and we could also, he felt, get some good fishing.

I must say I was immediately impressed by Ron Davis. He stood 6 feet 1 and was hung together by long muscles. He'd played end for the University of Florida, but he confided to me with a grin that college had done "durn little to get the cracker outa me." He struck me as the sort who'd make me feel like clearing out of the country in a hurry if I'd broken one of his pet laws. I was also greatly impressed when I got a look inside the trailer in which John Wilhelm was traveling. It was fitted out with practically every gun, fishing rod and variety of clothing and gear imaginable. With Davis, and Wilhelm, Bob Halmi, Mark Dichter and I joined forces and headed out on our mission.

As I talked with Ron, I tried to draw him out about what his worst problems might be. He didn't have any trouble deciding. He and numerous other wardens had an awful headache trying to deal with alligator poachers.

"With 'gator hides bringing at least six dollars a foot," Ron said, "and good ones going ten feet and more, it's easy to see why a pirate type wants to knock off every one he can."

This sort of poacher is a real outlaw, and generally has been raised as a lawless citizen. Certainly Florida is not the only state to have such types. And I presume in all fairness many of these poachers—people usually who are trying to scratch a living from the countryside—really believe they have a logical side to their breaking of the law.

Certainly nature helped the Florida poacher. It's almost as if much of the big swamp country was designed purposely for the kind of solitude the lawless life requires. Much of the coast is tattered by river mouths, estuaries, mangrove swamps and endless waterways. Where the fresh water meets the salt, an abundance of life flourishes. There are birds of endless variety. There are holes and springs known to natives where fishing is superb. There are bits of high ground near the wet expanses where a man can farm a little and guide in the off season. Thousands of such spots make perfect hideaways.

Perhaps it is touchy to intimate that any certain region has been populated by a rough element. But it is a fact—and many a Florida native will substantiate it—that numerous so-called "river rats" sought out an abode deep in some swamp while looking apprehensively over their shoulder. Thus it is no mystery why enforcement of game laws has been a problem. When one of a younger generation has been brought up to believe that the function of the country around him is to support him, it's hard to get the idea out of his head.

Although Ron Davis did not say so, I suspected as we visited that he realized there could be two sides. I imagine there are many cases where he wished he could do something about the poverty, about the misguidance by which a young fellow had grown up. Certainly many of the social problems of the region have been improved today. But a number of the present generation in the back country were raised by parents who knew real hunger. The easy money they got for helping bootleggers or poaching whatever they liked was a welcome find in an environment where there was little education and almost no chance to get ahead.

The first day at Crystal River, Ron and I fished. The weather was not too good for photography, so we decided to bide our time until it seemed better before going after the 'gator. Using jigs and shrimp, we caught many spotted weakfish, which natives here and elsewhere along the coast call "trout." As we fished, Ron told me about the illegal methods poachers use for hunting alligators.

Probably the most popular—and the hardest to stamp out—is that pursued by a hunter in a boat with a powerful spotlight. At night he cruises the swamps and waterways where he has previously located ample 'gator sign. Sweeping the spotlight around, at last he picks up on shore twin spots of glowing orange—a 'gator's eyes. Now he drifts close, shoots the creature between the eyes with a handgun or small rifle.

The skinning, for an old hand, is accomplished in a matter of minutes. The hide, salted on the spot, is rolled up and jammed into a flour sack. A rock or hunk of iron is tied to the bundle. If an approaching warden takes the poacher by surprise, it is a simple matter to slide the evidence over the side under cover of the darkness.

We changed locations several times as we fished. Ron called my attention to the endless maze of islands and channels. "It's next to impossible to surprise a poacher in a place like this," he said. "And to follow him at night is——well, forget it."

Unless someone has been in one of these places it's hard to visualize. Two or more channels will wind through the mangroves, interlaced with connecting waterways. At certain tides these connecting waterways may be nothing more than oyster bars, barely submerged. The underwater vegetation, and the way it might stream out in the water, makes the only clue for a guide as to whether or not he's in a main channel. It is pretty obvious that poking around these at night is some problem, indeed.

The next morning the light was good. We immediately decided to try filming the 'gator sequence. That is, if the hero of the show could be found. The weather was colder than we'd hoped for. At low temperatures alligators become sluggish, usually den up and are hard to find. Our schedule was so tight, however, that we had to take a chance.

The 'gator had last been seen in a bay which had, as an entrance, a narrow "throat" barely navigable at low tide. We were going to use Ron's airboat. As many visitors to the Everglades already know, this contraption is really something. An aeroplane propeller, mounted as a "pusher," powers the craft, which is steered by a rudder in the slipstream, just like a plane. Two seats, tandem, are mounted a good five feet above the hull. The height is necessary to give the driver a fair idea of what's in the water ahead. When they're going all out, about 50 mph, they draw less than 10 inches.

We loaded all the camera and sound gear into another boat. Ron and I had nothing but the gig we were to use, some spare rope, a roll of tire tape and a couple of bath towels to dry the 'gator's snout so the tape would stick when we taped his jaws closed. As Ron explained the operation, somehow this being a valet to an alligator didn't sound half as appealing for film material as it had before I got directly involved!

The gig was a long cane pole. On the end was a large, three-barbed, gang-hook with the hooks straightened out to form a harpoon. A line ran to this part. The hooks were about an inch and a half long. The outfit looked mighty flimsy to me, and I said so.

"If you gig a 'gator near his neck," Ron explained, "so that you can keep his head turned, you'd be surprised how well you can control one. As soon as the gig's planted, it pulls off the end of the pole and you have this Nylon line to hold him with."

"What if he gets into the shallows, and gets his feet on the bottom?"

Ron grinned. "You leap in and grab him."

"You don't say!" I was instantly wondering what

role *I* was to play in this wrestling match.

"One thing you must remember," Ron went on. "Stay away from that tail. It can break a man's leg like a match with one good swipe."

I mulled that over. "Why don't we just do a nice nature-type film? You know—the alligator in his primeval, undisturbed habitat."

Ron laughed. "Quit worrying," he said. "We may even live through this."

Ron told me as we weaved through the channels at a good 45 miles per hour that he'd had three complaints about this 'gator. "Complaint" or "nuisance" 'gators were, I gathered, one of a warden's biggest headaches. Most people are scared to death of the big reptiles. Actually the 'gator is pretty harmless. Perhaps one has been disturbed by the pressure of civilization and has moved overland to take up residence in a new lake or pond.

"Maybe such a 'gator winds up in a spot where there's a picnic ground," Ron explained. "Or maybe it's a lake used by a lot of water skiers. The minute somebody sees it, there's a howl."

Perhaps large alligators have harmed humans. But the incidents, if true, are at best obscure. The most common damage to man that has been documented occurs when a 'gator basking on a bank gets scared. Somebody comes along in a boat close to the bank. The alligator wants to get to the water and it probably senses that it is cut off. So, it doesn't do any intricate "thinking." It just bolts headlong, right over the top of the boat and whoever is in it, trying to get to the safe haven of deep water. Anyone in the boat could be seriously hurt by the flailing tail—if they weren't scared to death in the meantime.

As we approached the bay where this 'gator had last been seen, Ron cut the engine. We drifted up to a narrow spit of land that separated the bay from the channel. We both stood up, slowly. This gave us a pretty good view.

Ron seemed able to spot things everywhere. "Look at that big redfish," he said pointing. I was convinced he was seeing things, but there was a sudden wake as a big red bolted.

We could hear the other boat coming behind us. Ron said, "The 'gator may be on the bank. We'd better wait until we have the equipment set up because if he gets into the water and muddies up the bottom, we'll be out of business."

The bay was perhaps a hundred yards across. The channel leading into it was almost dry. Soon the other boat was next to us. Mark Dichter set up the sound equipment. Ron and I each had a radio mike around our necks so that our actual conversation could be recorded. Mark Dichter is the best sound man I know. He had us rigged so that we could go anywhere in the bay, trailing no wires, and still he'd have it all on tape.

Bob Halmi was going to have to wade with the camera. There were all sorts of whispered warnings to him about being careful not to step in a hole and douse the expensive gear. I began to feel that Bob's chore was certain to be at least almost as tough as mine. Later I wondered for some moments if it was not more so. There was better than half a mile of shoreline here on which the 'gator could be concealed, and we had to concentrate on every foot of it as if we were positive it was there. Since it had not been seen for 24 hours, of course it could be miles away.

We took a run at the "throat" of the bay and slid over. Ron was a master with that airboat. He handled it as if it were a toy. The boat could skid out, on a turn, like no other water conveyance I'd ever been on. He cut the engine and began quietly poling along the edge. In the distance we could hear shots and occasionally we'd hear the lisping of waterfowl wings. Whistlers, lesser scaup, mallards were flying overhead. But we paid little attention. We were tense.

Suddenly Ron pointed to a section of the tall grass about six feet back from the water's edge. "See that trail?"

I nodded. The grass was flattened as if a heavy body had been dragged over it.

"Hate to get Bob Halmi wet," Ron whispered—but his smile told me his hatred wasn't too strong —"but we'd better play it like we knew the 'gator was in there. The grass is bent as if it went inland."

We beckoned Bob in. He had a long, tortuous walk before he had got the camera close enough. It was cold and the bottom was rough. His camera, with a 400-foot magazine, was a big load. Meanwhile Ron had eased into the water. He moved gingerly to the spot where the grass was crushed. He peered off into the vegetation. Then slowly he raised his hand. He extended his index finger and made a motion ahead. Excitement poured through me. Ron's gesture could mean only one thing. He was looking at our quarry.

Moving slowly, quietly, Ron came back to the boat and started the engine. Then he leaped into the water, bolted up into the grass. I was confused. But not for long. In astonishment I saw him literally herding the 'gator toward the water, as if it were some variety of harmless livestock. The grass waved and billowed and suddenly there was the huge reptile. It looked around. Its snout seemed to me long enough to make up one whole alligator. But as it now slid into the water I was awed.

It seemed to go on and on. But swiftly. It moved far more swiftly than I had imagined. It must be 20 feet long, I thought, and I felt like calling everything off right then and there (actually it later measured 13½ feet). That is one whopper of an alligator, but I'd have sworn during those first seconds that it was much larger.

Ron bolted out of the grass, splashed into the water and leaped aboard. In a matter of seconds he had handed me the gig and started to chase the 'gator. The flat reflection of light on the water was giving him trouble. But when he momentarily lost the 'gator, he'd maneuver the airboat so that he was in easy striking distance of the bay's outlet.

For the first time now I was conscious of Halmi. Talk about guts. He was standing in the middle of that pond, his camera poised. To look at him you'd think the only company he had was a goldfish. I didn't envy him one bit. Nor did I have long to dwell on it, for just then Ronnie spurted toward one spot.

He blurted, "Get ready!" With great expertness he jockeyed us into position so that the light was good. I could make out the 'gator about a foot below the water. The boat zoomed in, overtaking the fleeing hulk. I had a good chance. I slammed the gig down. It hit the 'gator just in front of the powerful shoulders, at the base of the neck.

The pole broke. I was sick! A hunk of pole about a foot long was still stuck to the gig. If the 'gator rolled and mashed the hunk of pole against the bottom, it would tear the hooks free. But now I realized Ron had the Nylon line and he had it snug. He was maneuvering the boat close, and the hooks were holding. The next thing I knew Ron was yelling at me and handing me the line. And then he plunged overboard to mix it with the 'gator.

What happened next is somewhat of a blur. I'd heard that a man has no trouble holding the jaws of a 'gator clamped shut with one hand. But I was glad it was Ron proving the statement and not me. Together we finally bulled the 'gator on board in a wild melee of action. Several times it slugged the engine mounts with its tail and the whole boat shuddered. Ron kept yelling at me to watch that powerful tail.

I was doing my frantic best. Next thing I knew, Ron had the 'gator's head propped against his knee and was drying its jaw as though taking care of a child. Then he deftly taped the jaws shut and as swiftly as we could work we tied the 'gator with cotton ropes. At last it lay well secured in the bottom of the airboat. You could see a small mark where the gig had been.

Halmi went wild. He had shot every detail of the action. As the sun lowered we went buzzing home at full speed, shivering now, but happy with the success of our adventure.

Our next stop was to be on the other side of the state. We were to shoot film while hunting both quail and turkey. John Wilhelm had lined up a spot run by Bill Bonnette. Bill had been in the regular Navy and had fallen in love with Florida. He'd found a big ranch just northeast of Lake Okeechobee, owned by Stuart and Philip Iglehart of polo-playing fame, and he had leased it as a hunting preserve. Roughly 27,000 acres are in typical Florida rough-pasture country. This includes hammocks or high places, groves of cabbage palm, swampy spots and thick patches of brush. The palmettoes, especially where they've been cut once, make excellent quail cover and we had been assured we'd have good shooting. We piled everything into the Heli-Porter and took off. This plane is virtually perfect for our use. Strictly a STOL, (short takeoff and landing) aircraft with a big wing and beta control—whereby you can change the angle of the prop while landing and get the same effect as with variable flaps but without any porpoising— it will get in and out of almost any place. It will also haul a ton. If I'd designed a ship for our use I doubt if I could have thought of anything this Fairchild Heli-Porter doesn't have.

We made the flight across the state in about an hour, flew over the main hunting lodge, then dropped in to a strip less than a mile away. There was plenty of room in front of the lodge and, had I had a chance previously to search the ground for holes, I'd have plunked her right there. Later I did park it 30 yards from the main house. Ron Davis and John Wilhelm drove their vehicles over from Crystal River and they were a good five hours en route.

Bluefield, as the ranch is called, we found not pretentious but nonetheless everything for a hunter's comfort had been thought of. Bill Bonnette had some fine dogs. We hunted from Jeeps. There were so many quail I came near having a guilty feeling. We'd tool along, the dogs would point. We'd clamber out. Scent was so good the birds sat tight. On the covey rise Ron and I had great shooting.

Even though we'd see the singles down, we didn't hunt them too hard. The average covey was big, close to 20 birds. Bill wanted to leave them as large as he could so we concentrated on the covey rise, and left the singles alone. Now and then one of those would land in the open and not even try to make heavier cover. Bill would say, "Let's go after him. We'll be improving the breed by

Leg guards give hunter protection
against rough brush, as well
as snakes, when in the field in Florida.

dusting the ones that don't show too much sense."

Although the hunting was sensational, we had the built-in problem always present when trying to film this particular sport. The dog work is most dramatic. But when the quail flush, they are so small and so swift that the camera can seldom do them justice. The hunter present at the scene feels the drama, but whether the cameraman shoots in slow motion or normally, the birds just do not show up on the screen as the dynamic little gamesters they truly are.

There was plenty of fast action during
the quail hunting, with as
many as 20 birds in some coveys.

To round out our Florida show, we wanted to try for wild turkeys. John Wilhelm had a buddy, John Lee, who had a reputation as a wizard with a turkey call. To those who have never hunted wild turkeys, it must be explained that these birds are awesomely alert, wary, and adept at keeping their private lives private. They hear the slightest sound, practically see the grass grow. They seem always to have some sixth sense about where a hunter may be hiding. All of this is why the wild turkey has often been called the King of Game Birds.

Several methods of turkey hunting are popular and successful. One is to learn the habits of a particular group and try to waylay them on their rounds. Another is to use a call. In spring during mating season gobblers come well to a call imitating the talk of a hen. In fall they are not much interested in the sound of a call, whether it imitates hens or gobblers talking. Sometimes when a flock is first down off the roost in the dawn, they

63

can be called. This is because as each one flies down it alights somewhat scattered out from the others. All begin to talk and gather into a flock once more and then they start out feeding together. Also, if a turkey flock is frightened and scattered, and the hunter sits right down there and hides, then after a few minutes begins to work his call, quite often he'll get an answer and turkeys will come in to the sound. They are trying to group up once more.

We were faced, on the turkey hunt, with the ever-present hurdle one finds in filming game and hunting. At the time when the action is best, or at the only time when it is possible, often there is barely sufficient light to put an image on the screen. Bill Bonnette had selected a spot near a large swamp where turkeys had been coming off their roost to feed. This meant we had to start operations in the dimmest light of dawn. But I knew that Halmi, always expert with his camera work, would figure out some way to get the job done. During the afternoon before the hunt, we fashioned a crude blind, and another in the proper place for Bob and his camera. We were to roll out early and see what John Lee could do about calling a gobbler into range.

Those before-dawn roll-outs are all alike. You fight consciousness and hate every minute of it. But at last when you are out of your fog and settled in the outdoors, that hour before sunup is the most marvelous time of day. We crept silently to our blinds and got settled. We all but gave up breathing. We had to be utterly still.

Half an hour before light, when the east seemed to be pushing against the great purple canopy of the sky, various birds started moving. Several bunches of egrets, seemingly wanting to keep contact with the ground, flew over, barely clearing the blind. Two raccoons, looking like a couple of commuters off to catch the 7:12, trotted not six feet away. Bunches of ducks hurtled at us, their wings set for a landing in the swamp behind us.

Suddenly John Lee heard something. Ron nudged me. We felt John stir to get his call in action. Holding the cedar box in one hand, he rubbed the chalked striker across it, producing a low yelp. It ended on a higher note, making it sound almost like a question. It was so quiet afterward I could hear my own heart. Then there was a low answer from behind us.

Because of the light, we had to have our backs to the swamp. This added to the excitement. We dared not turn around to peek. Often when turkeys come to a call, one or two will sneak in so close the slightest movement in a blind spooks them.

They, in turn, flush the whole flock. I sat immobile. I felt all scrounged up. Something was tickling my nose. I thought I'd have to cough. Time wasn't dragging, it seemed to be going backward!

The suspense was literally awful. I had one small opening I could stare through. Suddenly something a bit darker than the surroundings I'd been unblinkingly staring at crossed this peep hole. I remember thinking that John surely ought to call again so the birds wouldn't leave us. But he waited, and I quit breathing. Then at last John yelped once more—and there was an answer that sounded as if it could not possibly be four feet from the blind.

Ron had his face pushed against the Spanish moss. He was touching me. He whispered, "Two gobblers. Ten o'clock. Take the one on your side." He nudged me to stand up.

As I arose I was conscious that the light was better than I had thought. And to my astonishment, turkeys were all around us. In one great wild flurry of winged panic, every bird flushed. They looked as big as F 100's.

I got my eye on the two Ron had seen. His gun boomed along the swamp. I saw his bird crumple and fall just as I squeezed off my shot. But my bird only rocked and went on. Even in my momentary frustration, I recall the thought crossing my mind that this was truly wonderful. Here we were within a mere 45 miles of Palm Beach, and in total wilderness, hunting the wariest game bird on earth. Fort Pierce, with over 25,000 people, was only 14 miles away. Yet as I watched that wounded bird still going, it was like being here way back when Ponce de Leon saw this country 450-odd years ago.

I was shooting again at the gobbler. But even as I did so I knew I had not reached it. Then a miracle seemed to happen. The gobbler suddenly crumpled and hit the turf. My first round had mortally wounded it. I bounded out of the blind with a warhoop and raced out to claim my prize. It was the perfect finish to a wonderful hunt.

Quail coveys were spread out, but the hunters used a Jeep and were able to move easily from cover to cover.

Alligator thrashes in shallow water
(opposite) as Joe aims with gig.
Top, Joe gigs the 'gator
which is later released
at Homasassa Springs, Florida (bottom).

Y O ranch near Mountain Home, Texas,

is stocked with exotic big game

such as the young eland opposite

and the fallow deer above.

Opposite top, herd of aoudad is

on the alert at Y O ranch.

Bottom, Joe, followed by Halmi,

stalks Indian blackbuck,

moving rapidly across the ranch (below).

# CHAPTER 9

# SAFARI FOR EXOTIC GAME IN TEXAS

It was an unbelievable scene. The broad valley stretched away before us and my thought was that this country, with its scrub liveoak, scattered cedar and cactus, its rocky draws and clumps of brown grass, might well pass for some scene from Africa or India. Far off on a hillside I could see a large tan animal standing beneath the wispy shade of a mesquite. Through my binocular it became a big bull eland. Down on the flat, moving along the edge of the brush, an oryx appeared, its tall, scimitar horns startling to see here.

That was just the beginning. Bobby Snow, who was our guide, said to me, "If you'll turn your glass over there to your right you can pick up a very excellent blackbuck. It just may be big enough

**Posing with his guide and the trophy aoudad which they bagged, Joe flashes a happy smile of success.**

for us to try, but it's much too far."

At last I had found it. The blackbuck, native of India, is a classic horned-game trophy. It is considered by many of the world's most experienced big-game hunters to have the most handsome head, compared to body size, of any of the world's horned game. The male of this particular animal, shining black along its back and down the outsides of its legs, with contrasting pure white below and running up the chest. was a stunning specimen. As I studied it my excitement was building, my heart beginning to pound. Then, atop a ridge to the left of the blackbuck, I suddenly saw a group of aoudad, or Barbary sheep, the goatlike animals originally of North Africa with a chest mane and furry leggings running down the front legs.

Bobby Snow was carefully studying the blackbuck. "It'll go maybe 19 or 20 inches," he said.

I knew that blackbuck have spiraling horns, with concentric rings also. "Do you measure around the spirals?"

"No," Bobby said, "I'm talking about length measured straight. A horn of 19 or 20 inches is good even in India. It is a fine head here."

Although it was difficult to fit what I was seeing into a pattern of reality, the fact was that we were not outside U.S. borders at all, but down in the middle of Texas. I have no doubt that many readers have heard of the famed Y O Ranch near

Mountain Home, Texas. Owner Charles Schreiner III, and ranch manager Vernon Jones, are widely known for the hunts offered at the 70,000-acre Y O for exotic big game of numerous species.

When we were making up a list of subjects we wished to cover for our program, THE OUT-DOORSMAN, Bob Halmi and I were both eager to put down as a must a hunt for one or two of the exotic, or foreign, big-game animals popular in certain places in the U.S. today. We began shopping around for an area where our hunt might be made to best advantage. The Y O Ranch seemed far and away the best all-round bet. With Mark Dichter, our ingenious sound man, we had flown from New York to San Antonio, Texas. There we were picked up by private plane and flown out the 100-odd road miles to the Y O, where we landed on a fine airstrip provided here.

Probably few readers realize just how great is the interest among U.S. hunters nowadays in hunting on big-game preserves such as the Y O, hunting, that is, for these introduced species. As everyone knows, the bird-shooting preserves have zoomed into popularity and there are now several hundred of them scattered across the U.S. Actually, the introduction of exotic big-game animals to a few places in the U.S. far outdates the founding of most of the bird-hunt preserves. But it is just over the past decade or so that herds have built up enough to allow much public hunting.

Years ago the Russian and European boar were brought to the U.S. by private clubs or wealthy land owners, and set free in large enclosures behind supposedly hog-proof fence. Some of these escaped and formed the basis for the hunting now well known in such places as Tennessee and North Carolina, portions of Texas, northern California, and even New Hampshire. The big Russian boars, it seemed, didn't pay much attention to fences.

But while the Russian boar hunting may have come first to public attention in the U.S., meanwhile a number of people, almost all of them in Texas, were experimenting with exotic horned and antlered game.

Probably the center of this occurred in Texas because it was here that the ranches were large. This offered the vast spaces needed for such game to thrive and multiply under virtually wild conditions. Also, the climate was conducive. A preponderance of the world's best and most acceptable trophies comes from moderate climes.

Another ultimate influence toward the boom in big-game exotics in Texas was the fact that Texas has almost no state, or public land. Hunting there has over many years grown into an almost totally commercialized proposition. I am not going to argue that this is either good or bad. I simply know that it exists, and that it works. I will say that commercial hunting for game both large and small is unquestionably what we in the U.S. are coming to eventually. Texas will have had such vast experience by the time it is accepted elsewhere that they will be ahead of the game.

At any rate, for as long as 30 years a few Texas ranches have had certain foreign big-game animals roaming their ranges. Under U.S. law, believe me, it is not any simple proposition to get started. You see, you cannot just hire some game trapper in India or Africa to catch a bunch of live wild animals and ship them to you. The reason is that the United States does not allow the importation of *any* new species except under federal strictures that are severe. The Fish and Wildlife Service, for example, has been searching the world in recent years for game birds to fill gaps in our terrain. When it decides to bring in a certain bird, specimens are officially turned over to one of the states to be propagated and then the progeny released. But big-game creatures—hoofed and horned animals—can only be brought to zoos.

Specimens are brought into port and quarantined for a specified length of time. Then they are taken directly to the zoo that has requested them. These particular specimens can never be released anywhere. They will spend the rest of their lives in a zoo. But, progeny born to these zoo animals, when surplus, can be sold. Thus, when the foreign big-game idea began to take hold in Texas, the big ranches had to get their original stock from zoo surpluses. When these animals, released on a particular ranch, multiplied, then under present Texas law there was no restriction on their sale.

A rancher could raise blackbuck and axis deer from India, sika from Japan, mouflon from Corsica, etc., and sell his own surplus live animals to others who might wish to start a preserve, or just raise a few for fun, or raise them to hunt.

The first magazine ads I ever recall seeing for hunting these exotics appeared about 15 years ago. They were placed by the Rickenbacker Ranch at Hunt, Texas, a rough, good-sized spread owned at that time by Eddie Rickenbacker and operated by his son, Dave. They offered axis deer, sika, black-buck, and the huge sambar deer from India, and they also had a few barasingha deer, as large as the sambar, from India.

Although there was apparently quite a lot of interest—and a good deal of hunting was done on this ranch—it changed hands several times, and seems to have been just a wee bit ahead of its time so far as national interest was concerned. The King Ranch, which allows no hunting, was quietly and without publicity raising numerous exotics, among them the nilghai or blue bull of India. Many other ranches, including the Y O, were gathering herds. Sika were being released along the eastern seaboard in several places, and are indeed publicly hunted in several spots there today. Fallow deer also were tried, in Kentucky, Alabama, Nebraska, and other places.

But, it was Charlie Schreiner at the YO, a working ranch started with cattle, sheep, mohair goats, and one of the country's best herds of authentic longhorns, who was looking ahead to crowded hunting conditions and seeing the really tremendous opportunities for commercial hunting of exotics. For one thing, you see, to date at least there are no season restrictions except those set by the preserve's owners. For instance, on that day as I stood glassing the blackbuck and working up a case of trophy fever, it was March. Whitetail deer season was long past. There was no public hunting of importance to be had anywhere in the U.S. But here, for a fee, we could hunt a dozen different big-game animals, and if we failed to kill anything, we would not have to pay.

"Pay only for what you kill" is the slogan of most of these preserves. Trophy animals run from $150 to $350 for average creatures such as blackbuck and mouflon. As herds build enough so that the larger animals such as eland and oryx, kudu, nilghai, and ibex are available, these may run as high as $600 to $1,500. Guide and transport and game care are furnished with the package. At preserves where lodging and meals are available, as at the Y O, the hunter pays extra for these.

*But, think what it costs to kill a polar bear, or a grizzly, or even an elk nowadays.* You can go to one of these exotics preserves and shoot a blackbuck, trophy guaranteed or no pay, for less than you can be guided to an elk on public land. And for that matter, you may go after the elk, spend your money, and still come home empty-handed!

Bobby Snow is a young man who is one of the resident guides at the Y O. He is an extremely experienced hunter, and he knows the ways of these foreign animals in great detail. He said now, "Do you think that blackbuck looks like what you want?"

"To me," I said, already panting a little, "it looks fabulous."

We got into the pickup and Bobby drove directly away from where we had seen the animal. He crossed a ridge, went bumping over rocks down a deep valley, turned back and came over another ridge to put us ahead of the animal, if it had continued its direction. He pulled up in a small thicket of liveoaks and put the pickup in the mottled shade where it would be difficult to detect.

He looked at me and grinned. "I don't know if you are like a lot of hunters who come here thinking these animals are tame. But let me tell you, this is no 'shoot-'em-in-the-barnyard' endeavor. I hope we can get you in range of that blackbuck. But I won't guarantee anything. They're wild, and I do mean!"

I did not really need to be convinced. We had seen groups of blackbuck does several times during the morning. Never did we see any of them standing. They were running when we spotted them, and way out of rifle range. Bobby had told me, laughing, that he believes blackbuck are born running. The does are tan colored. The bucks are also tan until they reach about 4 or 5 years of age. They then assume their mature coloring whence comes their name. They are awesomely swift, and extremely wary.

The argument as to whether or not these preserve animals are tame and "like shooting a cow in a feed lot" has been one of the hurdles that these big-game preserves have had to overcome. It is still a barrier of sorts, but it is slowly being broken down by the people who have tried this hunting. Actually, there isn't any argument. It is all a simple, cut and dried matter of how the animals are handled.

If you raise a whitetail fawn, or an elk fawn, in a pen, it will be as tame as your dog. If you raise it in a small pasture, it will be fairly tame, particularly if you feed it and it learns to come to feed each day. If you place it in a 100-acre pasture with gameproof fence, it may not be quite totally wild, but it will be so wild you won't be able to pet it, even if you feed it. The animals on a large place like the Y O are not under gameproof fence except in certain small breeding pastures where there is no hunting. They exist in a completely wild state. A blackbuck may be roaming a 1,000-acre pasture all its life, born there, right along with the whitetail deer and wild turkeys that are native. When you go deer hunting, you hardly ever cover a thousand acres in an entire hunt. Do you think the deer are tame? Hardly! Neither is the blackbuck.

Bobby Snow and I began our stalk. Bob Halmi and Dichter were going to try to set up where they could get any action on film and tape. We made our sneak up to the top, and peered carefully over. There was nothing in sight. We crept over the ridge, keeping to shadows of the small mottes of live oak, or dodging from small, stunted cedar to cedar. Then suddenly Bobby pointed and grabbed my arm.

The handsome blackbuck had been standing in a thicket of scrub oak, apparently watching us, from about 150 yards. It broke out in full flight. It is a fascinating, thrilling sight to see one run. This Indian antelope weighs on the hoof seldom more than 85 or 90 pounds. It looks larger, but is exceedingly trim. It runs with no effort, and at astounding speed. It can also jump. It is not much of a fence jumper, but has a habit of running and then suddenly sailing straight up. As it does so it folds its legs up tightly under its body. Thus it appears to be sailing far up and for a distance of possibly 20 feet, legless. To see a whole band turn this trick is an astonishing experience. Several small does and a younger, tan buck with shorter horns had popped up seemingly from nowhere and now the entire band was coursing off through the scattered scrub.

We tore back to the pickup and raced at crazy speed down the pasture on a dim ranch trail. Bobby was hoping the animals would circle and that we could get in position for a shot at nominal range. If you want a real thrill, just take a ride with any of the guides or with Schreiner or Vernon Jones sometime. The vehicles, most of them, are four-wheel drive, and equipped with two-way radio linked to ranch headquarters and each other. I had one ride with Charlie Schreiner when he was wheeling at 40 miles an hour cross-country, dodging among scrub live oaks, hitting the dead ones head on so that they flew in a clatter over the top of the vehicle. Rocks, down stuff, he didn't even slow up for—and all this time he is talking to another car and to headquarters on the radio, driving with one hand. No wonder Texans get the kind of all-out hell-for-leather publicity they do.

Now Bobby slid to a stop and literally shoved me out. I got my Remington 7mm. magnum ready and Bobby said, "That band should cross the trail right down here ahead about 75 yards. Get set!"

I hunkered down. I snugged the rifle to my shoulder. I looked through the scope, tensely watching the trail.

"Shoot him!" Bobby yelled.

Zip. That blackbuck had come from nowhere, and in a split second of here-he-comes, there-he-goes, he had shot across the narrow ranch trail like an arrow released from a bow. All four feet were off the ground as he literally flew across. I imagine he was traveling at least 50 miles an hour.

I got up, heart hammering and breath coming in gasps. "Shoot him?" I gulped, with a questioning look at Bobby. "Good Lord, man, I hardly had time to *see* him!"

I didn't know it, but Halmi and Dichter had been right there backing us up. They howled in glee. "The first person who asks you if these animals are tame," Bob said in one of his infrequent moments of hilarity, "you ought not to answer— just hit 'im!"

We had a lot we wanted to film around the headquarters, and so next day we concentrated mostly on that. The Y O Ranch is one of the old and important ranches in Texas. Although Charles Schreiner III now lives in San Antonio most of the year, he and his family maintain a handsome home at the Y O. His mother also has a lovely part-time home there. So does Vernon Jones, the ranch manager. Don't get the impression that this is a dude ranch. It isn't. Around the headquarters region, which comprises perhaps 100 acres, there are houses where some 23 resident cowboys live. Real, honest-to-goodness cowboys. Some of them are among the finest riders and ropers I have ever seen. Some are Mexicans who speak little English, and of those a few are second or third generation, born here, as were their fathers.

There is a resident biologist, full-time employee, Charlie Land, who with his family lives in the headquarters area. Charlie is game manager. Including the hunting in season for whitetail deer, several thousand animals are harvested on the Y O annually. This is truly a big business, and an interesting one. People from all over the world have come here to hunt, and do come each year.

We wanted to get some film of the longhorn herd. Charlie Schreiner organized and is president of the Longhorn Breeders Association, which now has grown to national proportions. Its purpose was to preserve the longhorn, which Charlie's grandfather raised, and which was until several years ago so close to extinction that it was in a most precarious situation. Now there are numerous herds, and Charlie and his organization were successful in getting it listed as a registered breed, with full specifications as to what conformation it should have.

We were also vastly intrigued by the cottage where we were staying, and by the others that are currently used to house guests who wish to stay at the ranch while hunting. Charlie is a collector of all sorts of things, from Wells Fargo items to old guns to log cabins. Yes, I mean that, log cabins. He has searched Texas for log cabins dating back many years, has bought several well over 100 years old. Among them is the Sam Houston. These he has had taken down log by log, with each piece numbered so it could be reconstructed. Then, at the Y O headquarters, these have been rebuilt, with modern touches here and there so that the interiors are beautiful and functional yet with the precise atmosphere of the original. Charlie has been officially recognized and lauded in many quarters for his preservation of history in this useful manner.

On the porch of the Sam Houston cabin where we stayed, Bobby Snow called our attention to a number of fine game heads, all exotics. It fairly made me drool as we started out next day. That blackbuck had crossed me up so badly that I really had my neck bowed today. But secretly, I didn't know how I would ever be able to kill one. Or, for that matter, an aoudad either. We had spent the remainder of the previous day trying to sneak up on a good aoudad. We had spotted a dandy, with one horn I guessed at myabe 26 inches. But when the big devil turned his head— the other horn was broken to about 10 inches long. I just held off squeezing the trigger in time to save collecting a trophy we certainly would not have wanted to take.

It is always curious to me how, in big-game hunting, things go badly, or seem impossible. And then, all of a sudden, in a split second when one is least expecting success—it is there. We were in a rather dense area of small brush and oaks. Bobby and I were carefully skulking along, glassing here and there at intervals. Halmi and Dichter came behind us, and I knew it was hard, hot work for Bob to carry the heavy camera with its big magazine.

One moment the ridge across from us was bare except for trees. In the next, a beautiful tableau appeared almost magically. Five fine aoudad rams in a single group simply seemed to arise from out of the grass and pose there, sky-lined. Probably they had been coming up from the other side. They stood now as if each had been placed in position by someone forming up the group to look its best for a picture. Each turned its head and against the blue of the sky the great horns, sweeping out and back and down across their shoulders, made an inspiring sight.

I was so afraid this mirage would disappear. I moved close to a tree to try to get a rest. There was no time to use my binocular. I had to scan them with my scope.

Bobby said, "The one that this minute is in the middle is best. I think about 22 inches. They get larger, but he is a very good ram indeed."

I glued my eye to the big fellow and never re-moved it. The group broke up and trailed down on the side of the ridge we were looking at. Then the one Bobby Snow had picked for me turned broadside, cocked his big head. I could see the fringe of chest mane and his leggings, and as I squeezed and the report laced across the valley, the others bolted. My trophy just seemed to sink into the grass and disappear. That 7mm. Remington magnum packs a terrific punch. I was elated. Just like that, in seconds, the big fellow had been collected. I had not even had time to start shaking!

Somehow, after that, although we glassed many animals and had endless thrills looking at the great variety of them, the blackbuck was almost anti-climactic. We had jumped so many whitetails while hunting blackbuck, and I knew by now that, difficult as a whitetail deer can be, I could have killed a dozen while trying for a single good blackbuck. But then at what seemed like almost the time when we'd have to give it up, everything jelled.

There was a handsome big fellow racing like the wind. It swept behind a shallow ridge and I knew there was not a chance of ever seeing it again. I did not even bother to get ready. Then to our amazement the animal came wheeling back over the same ridge, circling, and as we stood utterly still it circled clear around and came within modest range. It hauled up, looking back over its shoulder at a small group of little tan does trotting along behind. What a regal mien this dapper antelope had. I put the crosshair on and sucked in my breath. It occurred to me then that Bobby had not said a word.

"Am I right?" I asked tensely. "Is it good enough?"

"You're right," Bobby Snow said. "But you'd darn well better hurry. He's going to go."

The buck gathered its muscles. At that instant the Remington spoke to it and it obeyed the command, folding without so much as a quiver.

Later that evening we sat in the Chuckwagon, the small restaurant operated on the premises where all of the cowboys, the guides and guests eat wonderful, plain "cowboy cookin'." Charlie Schreiner was there and questioning us about how it had gone.

"Just tell me," he said. "Did you enjoy it? Does preserve hunting for exotic big game suit you?"

"Charlie," I said, "let me put it this way. It sure is one heck of a lot cheaper than going to India or Africa. But now you tell me—couldn't you get 'em a little bit less wild? From what I hear, it's easier than this by far on their native grounds."

# CHAPTER 10

# FATHER AND SON PACK TRIP IN COLORADO MOUNTAINS

The trail was very steep and with numerous terraces. The horses had to make short bursts of speed in spots to gain momentum enough to get to the top. Then we'd pull up and let them blow a bit, meanwhile looking down for what seemed an endless swirling, dizzy distance to a tiny ribbon of sparkling blue that was Colorado's Los Piños or Pine River, far below. After a pause we'd start up the slope once more, climbing slowly mile after mile. We were in the San Juan Wilderness Area, making a pack trip up to the high country where lay a group of small glacial lakes filled with fat trout. All I could think of was that the scenery was unbelievable, and how could Bob Halmi possibly tell, with his camera, the tremendous thrill of just being here. There was too much to possibly even comprehend.

I turned to my 15-year-old son, Frank, who was riding immediately behind me, and said, "What do you think?"

"Terrific," he said. "It practically makes me short-winded to look at it."

Behind Frank, next in line, was Bob Halmi's youngster, Kevin, also 15. Funny thing, when we had first talked about a father-son pack trip into the mountains somewhere, we'd not had the slightest idea of putting it on film. You see, my boy rates as a westerner, having spent most of his time in South Dakota. Bob Halmi is a New Yorker,

and his boy is an authentic easterner. Neither of the boys had been on a high-country horseback trip, and it seemed a little bit ridiculous. Here Bob and I were making our living doing our OUTDOORSMAN TV series and traveling all over the map into all sorts of stand-on-end country, and yet it just seemed we never got a chance to ring the kids in on a thing. We needed to spend more time together doing such things, now that they were teenagers. Time goes awfully fast.

We had just completed a really tough trek and were talking about some sort of vacation. "Why don't we take the boys on a pack trip?" I said to Bob.

He snorted. "A mailman's vacation—take a walk!"

"No," I told him, "I'm serious. Let's take Frank and Kevin and go somewhere in the mountains and ride up and camp and fish some. Just laze around and get acquainted. It is preposterous that here I'm a fisherman and don't get time to teach my own son the fine points."

Bob was slowly won over to the idea. But as we talked about it, I began to suspect that Bob, who is an all-business sort and just can't quit, was seeing film possibilities, too. Then the first thing I knew, I was getting excited over the idea.

Let me explain it this way. Sure the grizzly hunts and the fast-action stuff are great. But every year thousands of fathers and sons dream of riding off into the wilderness and doing some fishing and getting acquainted. There is just as much drama and excitement and enjoyment in the more slowly paced pastime of riding up into the 11,000-foot country and fishing for modest sized trout in a wilderness lake, as there is in shooting an elephant.

Suddenly Bob and I found ourselves not talking vacation at all. We were talking enthusiastically about taking these young fellows up into the mountains somewhere and putting the experience on film for our series, so others might enjoy it vicariously. Maybe, too, others would get the idea to go and do likewise before their kids are grown up and gone.

In June of 1967 I drove from Phoenix and Bob and our sound man Mark Dichter from New York. Both Bob and I had a boy in tow. We had after much pondering and research hit upon the idea of spending a day or so at a dude ranch and combining it with a pack trip. In shopping around for a place that appeared to offer precisely what we wanted, we discovered Wilderness Trails Ranch out of Bayfield, Colorado. We both homed in from opposite directions to Durango, and there Mickey Craig, the owner of Wilderness Trails, picked us up and drove us the short hop out to the ranch.

I must confess that as we drove from Bayfield, a small southwestern Colorado village, out north toward Mickey's dude ranch, I was beginning to wonder. The country was beautiful, but it looked to me a little bit like farm country. Here the Pine River rollicks along, on its way to pour into Navajo Reservoir in northern New Mexico, at its confluence with the San Juan. But presently we came to Vallecito Reservoir, formed by a dam on the Pine, and the country changed rather abruptly. We were in tall pines, the road was narrow and snaking around the juts of steep cliffs. Presently we passed the upper end of this reservoir, left the resort spots that are numerous along its shores. The pavement ended, and we were bumping along on a Forest Service road.

This looked better, I'll tell you. I guess I have just lived so long in the back-country areas that the wilder it gets, the better I like it. At last we came to a gate that said in large letters: WILDERNESS TRAILS RANCH. The road here was too narrow to meet anybody, strictly a one-way trail. On our right the brawling Pine, full of huge boulders and roaring white water and as inviting a trout stream as I ever saw, poured along so close we could all but touch it. Spruce and pine marched along beside us. Mountains rose in arrogant, breathtaking cliffs on either side. Ahead, each

time the vista opened up a bit, there was a fabulous view. We were staring, without knowing it, straight into the brooding, vast high area of the San Juan Wilderness into which we were eventually to pack.

Wilderness Trails is a spot so inviting, so pleasant it is difficult to describe. A mile or so from the gate, the valley broadened a bit. A log bridge led us across the river, and here a handsome big log lodge stood, surrounded by log cabins all but hidden in the pines. We could see a horse corral and barns, with horses scattered here and there. Two big St. Bernard dogs came out to woof at us in friendly welcome as we pulled up by the lodge. Presently we had been introduced to Mary Ann Craig, Mickey's wife, a hostess with a manner so casual that one is instantly at ease.

A portion of this place, we were to learn, was Colorado's first and therefore oldest dude ranch. Although the Craigs do not operate that part today, it lends an aura that, along with the ancient and inspiring mountains, seems to surround the place with taste and dignity and yet with the most relaxed atmosphere that I have ever seen in such an operation. Everyone, we learned, does about as he pleases. The organized activity of trail rides, cook-outs, evening square dances, fishing in a private and well-stocked trout pond or in the Pine River, or just hiking and lounging and getting fat on the excellent food—all of this is so deftly organized to seem "unorganized" that you hardly know you are being led around and pampered.

Mickey Craig is a tall, slender, handsome gent who looks as if he must have just stepped off a horse and out of an ad for western wear, or else that he is some hero of western films who surely you must know. He was itchy to get going immediately. Previously it had been raining and snowing up high, he told us. He hoped we could make our trip while a bit of fair weather was on.

I said, "No, you don't, Mickey. This started out to be a vacation, originally, before we talked ourselves into a film. So at least we have to fiddle around the ranch a day or so before taking off."

We did just that. But it was evident that with the adventure of the high country calling, regardless of the fun and comforts here we were all eager to start "up the hill."

It is quite a chore for an outfitter to get everything ready for a party to move into the mountains and camp. We met our horse wranglers, young fellows from Texas who had taken summer jobs up here and were used to riding. One, I learned, had been riding bulls in amateur rodeos for some time, so a string of horses didn't give him much trouble. We met the cook who would go up with us. And then one morning the boys brought the pack string and our mounts. Bob, Mark and I somehow got all our gear packed aboard. With the wranglers, cook, and Mickey Craig, we all started up the Forest Service road, finally came to Granite Peaks camp ground, and from here we left the last possible contact with civilization and started up the rough and winding trail to Emerald Lake.

Part of the excitement of a trip like this, particularly with the boys along, was looking for wildlife and being overwhelmed by the scenery. There was plenty of that. This towering country had clouds hanging in gossamer strands here and there. Occasionally a quick, cold little rain squall hit us. Immediately afterward the sun burst out.

We paused now and then while the wranglers tightened cinches. One of them was working on my son's saddle and he said, "This old nag always swells her belly up when you saddle her. She does it so she can relax then and the cinch won't feel tight." He put his knee against her belly and gave a heave. She grunted and turned her head to try to nip at him. He grinned up at me. "That'll fix her."

I knew as I watched Frank and Kevin that the riding was a great enjoyment for them. I guess I have got to the point where certainly I'd rather ride a horse than walk, but, as many a rancher says, "I avoid a horse as much as possible."

I was smirking to myself along about noon when I watched both boys get down and walk around. It was dead certain their backsides were going to be well worn before we got up on top and to camp. They'd likely be lame, too. I watched the easy, relaxed flat-in-the-saddle way the wranglers rode. I thought to myself: "What a shame it is that so many young people have to live in cities nowadays and never know the casual feel of a saddle or a pack." But that's how civilization is nowadays, I guess, and we are fortunate we have wilderness areas to go into on occasion. It is a way to "get well" in both mind and body, even though you may get a little bit lame in the process!

Late in the afternoon we were working along a little draw where aspens grew and a sparkling creek tumbled. There was a small mountain park on the slope. Suddenly I noticed Kevin's horse swing its head that way and throw its ears forward. Then Mickey, up ahead, raised a hand and motioned us to stop and be silent. Over at the edge of the mountain meadow there was a small band of elk. We were in shadow and had the breeze in our favor. We'd not been detected.

We watched them now, both boys very much intrigued and excited because neither one had ever seen wild elk like this before. The animals fed along, raising their heads occasionally. One, a bull, had the beginnings of antlers, but of course they were in velvet and just getting well started at this season. Nonetheless, it was a tableau that stamped this place as total wilderness, and we were all glad for the interlude. A bit farther on a fat mule deer bounded across the trail a short distance ahead.

"The muleys," I told the boys, "have it great. You know, most of them live all summer way up here, many of them in groups far up around timberline. What a life. Nothing disturbs them. They have almost no enemies—an occasional lion or bear, or maybe an eagle manages to grab off a fawn. But really it is a life to be envied. It's not until heavy snows come that they drift down to lower elevations. This is one of the few animals in our country that makes, in the high mountain country, what is called a 'vertical migration'— up with the spring, down when winter strikes."

Emerald Lake was beautiful. It lies among the high crags, with the usual close-to-timberline boulders and rocks, the lovely mountain meadows with scattered flowers practically springing from snowbanks. I asked Mickey about other lakes.

He said, "If we had time we could go to a new one every day. There is Elk Lake, and on over the divide from there about a twelve-mile ride there's Ute. All of these high lakes have cutthroat or rainbow trout. They have to be stocked by plane, they're so inaccessible."

We spent until well after dusk getting settled in camp and just getting ourselves oriented. The boys wanted to try the fishing, but they had not reckoned with the pickiness and selectivity of high-country trout. They came back to the campfire discouraged and troutless. By then, however, the cook had a wonderful, ample but plain meal run up for us. The wranglers had the horses taken care of. We all gathered around and filled up too full on everything and now lounged around the campfire, each one of us getting better acquainted with the other, the silent wilderness an amalgam that knits groups

**Much of the fun of a pack trip is the excellent trout fishing in the high country's streams and lakes.**

together as nothing else can.

I presume each of us, in telling our tales by the campfire, exaggerated a bit. I was as big a hero as I could make out, Halmi had had dangerous experiences all over the world that just might have been toned down a bit. Dichter and his sound equipment had been harassed by untold difficulties, and Mickey related how a gun had blown up in his face, and how he had fallen on rocks in a Texas hunt, smashed his rifle and almost been killed. It was wonderful.

All of this, too, you see, is part of the great outdoors and its experience. It was like being hopped up on the greatest narcotic ever invented —crystal air, the scent of the forest, the overwhelming silence and vastness of the wilderness. The cook related experiences we'd never have guessed. The young bull-riding wrangler told a few that maybe were enhanced just a wee bit, should we say, by imagination. Our own kids let go with derring-do we'd never even imagined.

At dawn I had both boys down on the lake shore, shivering in the chill, which was almost down to freezing. I had set up Shakespeare spin rods for each of us to begin with. I was determined not only to get in some fishing but to make this trip educational to both boys as well. It would be something they'd never forget, and might use many times in life.

I worked them hard on fine points of casting, trying to teach them from out of my own experience. I explained how high-country trout do not have a wide choice of food. Life in the glacial lakes is sparse. Terrestrial insect life up at this altitude is not as varied as lower down. Thus, the trout grow up utilizing only certain kinds of food, and they become extremely whimsical. The spoons and spinners struck by trout in the lower altitude lakes and streams are a puzzle to these fish.

"That doesn't mean they won't ever hit a spoon like Frank is using," I said.

At that moment he set back on the rod. The tip arced down and a bright silvery trout shot out of the water. "I guess it doesn't!" Frank yelled happily. He worked on the trout, taming it. And presently Kevin also had one. I knew right now it would be difficult to get those boys to do anything else—like doing their stints before Bob's camera to depict the general routine. They had been hooked by the fishing.

That noon we had trout fried crisp and brown for lunch. Lots of it. After lunch the boys and Bob and I took a short ride, just looking around for items of interest. Up a small creek we discovered something that grabbed the interest of both boys

again. Here was a series of small ponds, each formed by a perfectly engineered beaver dam.

"I didn't know beavers lived up this far in the mountains," Kevin remarked.

"Sure," I told him. "The odd thing is that early trappers found beavers virtually all over the U.S. from high to low. They were trapped by the thousands, of all places, along the Rio Grande and its tributaries, on what's now the Mexican border. They were also found in northern Florida, and throughout all of the North right on up to the tree limit. The only places where there are no records of them were southern Nevada and southern California."

We spent a long time examining the small holding dams, some only three or four feet wide, on rivulets below the main dam. As at last we turned to leave the larger pond, there was a big splash at its upper end. We whirled around and there was the circle made by a beaver that had just taken fright and dived. Had we been watching closer we'd probably have seen it. And it no doubt had been trying to puzzle out what sort of creatures we were.

Next day Mickey thought we should ride to another lake to give it a try. We made a trip to Elk Lake. This was my chance to get the boys started fly fishing. All of us eagerly pushed down the steep slope to where this bright blue glacial jewel lay, and as soon as rods could be put together and strung we were starting. I felt that in such a setting the boys should really learn how to do this expertly. I started them out with 3-ounce, 7-foot Shakespeare fly rods. I gave them some pointers on how to use the wrist for the power of the cast, not try to flail out the line with arm motion. I showed them how, in picking up a cast, you imagine you're going to throw the line straight up with a flick of the rod. Of course you can't. It goes out behind in a long U. But imagining you will toss it straight up cures you of bringing the arm back too far.

"Just about to one o'clock is far enough back," I explained. "Let me show you another trick, too."

I explained that many times one gets into a spot where the back cast has to be kept fairly low, the U a "tight" one, not a large, wide loop. "You bend your wrist in a shorter, more snug motion as you make your forward cast," I explained. "That keeps the line in a thin U and out of branches, let's say, that may be right above your head. Of course, if there are obstructions close behind you use the roll cast . . . like this." I demonstrated for them.

Frank said, "Dad, how about us catching a trout now instead of going to school all day?"

There is an exciting variety of wildlife to be
seen in the remoteness of the mountains
—like the porcupine, above, and the skunk, below.

Everyone laughed, and we got down to business. We tried dry flies, because a few trout were intermittently rising. But as long as the surface stayed smooth, not a trout would touch our offerings. When suddenly a small breeze riffled the surface, there was a swirl at Frank's fly and he was fast to a nice cutthroat. It wallowed, then fought deep and hard. By the time he had got it ashore another riffle swept across the water and Kevin had one. Then I did, too. I surmised this was because the clear surface showed our leaders too plainly, but I later discovered the wind was blowing insects out of the towering spruces nearby and the trout came up to dine whenever the wind blew.

They were handsome fish. I showed the boys the twin red slashes under the chin that gave these trout their name. I explained that the cutthroat was the trout native originally to most of the West, and that the rainbow, native originally only on the west slope, had been stocked far and wide but had not always been even in lakes like this.

Our last night in camp I lay in my sleeping bag knowing we were going to have to go down the mountain next day, and I wished somehow that we could just stay on and on. One more day, and another . . . and never return to civilization. I stirred a bit and one of the boys spoke to me and then the other.

Bob said, "You all better get some sleep." But I knew that each of us was having his own thoughts, and regrets that we were going to have to go. It had been a wonderful experience.

As we snake-tracked down the trail next day, one of the wranglers pointed to a spot in the timber and called out to Bob, "You want to photograph a porcupine?"

The whole pack train stopped then and there. Halmi was tearing around to get equipment, the boys were sliding off their mounts to go have a look. Now we could all see the animal, comically lumbering, and as we surrounded it, it switched its big, thorny tail angrily to warn us, while keeping its head hunched low. It was the western variety, usually called "yellow haired porcupine" because the long guard hairs above the quills are yellowish.

We had one more big thrill coming before we got back to the ranch. In an area of pines lower down, not far from the river, where a scattering of openings and meadows ran, Mickey held up a hand to keep us all quiet.

He dismounted in the timber and said, "I've seen some coyotes in this area. They feed on mice and other small animals around these meadows. Would you like to see if we can call one up?"

The boys were instantly full of questions about how this is done. While the wranglers and cook stayed with the horses, we all made a silent hike far around, watching the wind, and at last Mickey motioned for us to hide. He sat at the base of a big tree, screened by branches, took a coyote call from his pocket and began to blow it. The anguished wail poured across the meadow. It was supposed to imitate the squall of an injured rabbit.

He paused, and in a few moments repeated again. This he did over and over, looking at his watch to make sure he stayed at it long enough.

We had been there exactly 15 minutes and I knew everyone was getting itchy. The boys' expressions said plainly that they thought Mickey was pulling their leg. Then I saw Mickey freeze, bring his hand slowly to his mouth, and squeak very low, making the sound with lips pressed to his palm. I followed with my glance where he was staring. Over there at the edge of the meadow a big tawny-gray coyote was standing immobile, looking toward where we crouched.

Mickey squeaked again. Very low. The animal made a little run ahead and paused once more, testing the breeze. Both boys were utterly flabbergasted as they stared at the scene. Now the animal circled, as they always do, to try to get the wind on the place from which the sound emanated. We watched it lope around and into the timber. That was that. We never saw it again. It had circled until it picked up our scent, and then had fled in terror.

The experience was a fitting climax to our trip. That evening, bone-weary, we all sat around the table in the big lodge, filling up on the fine food put out by the head chef. Mary Ann Craig and her handsome family of small children were gathered around, listening to our experiences. I sat there thinking that drama and enjoyment are of many kinds.

We had not killed any huge game animal. Nothing had attacked us, nor had we even been mildly challenged. We had fought no huge fish, slain no dragons.

Yet in satisfaction this trek into the high-country wilderness had amply measured out everything we could possibly have desired. It had also for a short time placed a couple of dads and their sons closer together and let them see each other in new perspectives against the ever-neutral backdrop of nature. I found myself hoping that every father and son in the whole country might have opportunity at least once to trace a path like we had into the wilderness.

# CHAPTER 11

# HOW TO STALK GAME WITH CAMERAS
## By Robert Halmi
### PHOTOGRAPHS BY THE AUTHOR

As most readers of this book will already know, Joe Foss and I are partners in the production of THE OUTDOORSMAN. I am the cameraman. Although Joe gets to enjoy all of the thrills of shooting with a gun, there are plenty of thrills for me, too. The camera can indeed be a most exciting "weapon" to use in hunting and fishing, and many of my experiences in shooting film have, I'm sure, been far more dramatic for me than I could possibly have found by trading places with Joe.

I think as I write of an evening when the light was swiftly fading in a forest in British Columbia. Joe and I were hugging the trunk of a big spruce and listening intently. My movie camera was out of film, but as always I had a still camera slung about my neck. There was a small stream nearby and the sounds we were listening to were of rocks being turned over. A grizzly was over there rooting around, apparently looking for grubs or other food beneath the rocks.

Suddenly there was an unusual crash of rock on rock. Joe stirred and I heard a click as he let off the safety on his Remington. Now he sucked in his breath and whistled, a long, low note. Willows a short distance before us along the stream bank were about three feet high. Above them now the great bear reared. It stood upright, weaving on its hind legs, trying to identify the sound.

A shaft of late, yellowish sunlight gently crossed the animal's head. The silver-tipped hairs around its neck were thus lighted in such detail that they looked almost as if magnified. My instinct told me instantly that I must "shoot" this bear. I knew I had the Nikon shutter set at only 1/60th second and wished I had had it faster, because I did not dare lose time. A 60th is slow for game that may move suddenly. However, I braced my shoulder against the spruce to steady myself, and was thankful at least that the camera was loaded with high-speed film.

As I looked through the range finder I saw a terrific picture. There was more here than I had noted at first glance. A trace of evening mist was catching light behind the bear. This accentuated the relative depth of the scene. All objects stood out as if in third dimension, even on the flat plane which the camera would see. I was filled with excitement, not thinking at all, I'm sure, of any possible danger. This striking picture was here and I had to get it before it disappeared.

I started shooting as fast as I could cock the camera. I banged out six frames, and then the bear, apparently satisfied that nothing worth bothering with was here, dropped onto all fours and ambled away. Next to me I heard Joe let out his breath with a *whoosh*.

Now then, I've hunted with a gun in many

places over the world, and have shot a fair number of animals. After a long stalk, it is certainly exciting to collect a trophy. But now as I looked at the narrow stream, and reflected that I had been shooting the pictures with a 105mm. lens (a medium telephoto) and that the bear had filled the frame, I realized that the animal could not have been more than 25 yards' distant. I had just enjoyed a thrill that certainly could compare with any I've had hunting with a rifle. Already anticipation to see the processed picture was nagging me. Had I held the camera still enough? Had I used proper settings? I could hardly wait to get a look at the result.

Because I have been a professional photographer for many years, it is somewhat difficult for me to see things through the eyes of the average camera buff. Yet I suppose we both have about the same basic reactions. The satisfaction of having brought home some good pictures can certainly last as long, or longer, than the rewards from any other pastimes or occupations. But probably the real drive to keep on shooting, shooting, shooting is the nagging feeling that the next photo may somehow be better. This constant attempt at improvement is a tremendous stimulant.

For me, viewing each picture is a way of reliving the heart-in-the-throat moment when I squeezed the shutter release. With wildlife pictures in particular, capturing an animal alive and at home in its own special environment is a tremendous satisfaction.

Just consider, too, that one can do this with a camera that cost less, often, than it would to mount the same trophy. There are no permits, no licenses to buy. There are no closed seasons, no fully protected species. You can "shoot" females. No matter where you travel, there is always wildlife of some variety. Often the protected species offer the best and most rewarding opportunities, because they are more likely to be rare, or at least not abundant. Indeed, the cameraman has a far greater latitude, and many more opportunities to "shoot," than does the gunner.

During the filming of the various episodes of THE OUTDOORSMAN: JOE FOSS, some of which are described in this book, we took many still pictures. Mostly these were thought out to tell a part of the story of filming the TV series. Much of what I do in taking such photos is quite comparable to what will happen to *any* photographer, under similar circumstances. Equipment techniques I must use are much the same as those *you* will use if you pursue wildlife photography as a hobby.

Of course, I must usually carry *more* equipment, but the basics all fall into about the same general pattern. There is not room here to give any long course in outdoor photography. But perhaps some of the things I've learned—often at the expense of much time and wasted film—will be helpful to others.

I would suggest that you use a camera of the single-lens reflex type that takes 35mm. film. This type of camera will offer you the widest latitude in adding lenses. There are a few single-lens reflex cameras in the 2¼ x 2¼-inch size also, but these are rather bulky and awkward, and much more expensive as regards the film they gobble up. In my view, they offer no real advantage over the 35mm. film format.

There are many good SLR 35mm. cameras in a wide range of prices. I would advise against buying extremely cheap ones. Get a decent camera of some well-known brand, then you can be sure of obtaining good service if you ever need a repair or adjustment. This camera will have a so-called "normal" lens of probably 50mm. which produces pictures about as the human eye views a scene. Probably, you'll need to add auxiliary lenses, how many depending on how much money you can spend, your needs, and how much weight you think you can carry without handicapping your opportunities.

For good hunting, fishing and wildlife photography, certain basic lenses are absolutely indispensable. These lenses will be wide angle and telephoto. The former let you "take in" a great deal more area than the normal lens will cover. To reach out you need telephotos which magnify and bring distant objects and wildlife closer.

One great advantage of a wide-angle lens is that its focus is not critical. It has great depth of field. Thus, using a wide angle, you can work very closely behind a hunter or fisherman, peering over his shoulder so to speak, yet taking in the whole action scene with everything in acceptable focus. For work in a boat, for instance, a wide-angle lens is practically mandatory when the fishing action starts. The normal lens will not cover enough space to allow you to cope with your cramped quarters.

There are differences of opinion about how far to go with wide-angle lenses. A very acceptable compromise is to outfit with a 35mm. wide-angle. This will serve most average needs. However, a 28mm. will perhaps be more to your liking. It has vast scope and depth. You must remember, however, that as a wide-angle gets "wider" it tends to distort lines that are close to it. Thus if you are sitting low in a canoe using a 28mm. lens, it is possible that some pictures may seem to show the canoe much "fatter" in the middle than it is. Since everything else in the picture will be in proportion, however, the fault is not a serious one, and is immensely offset by the advantage of sharpness offered by this type of lens. Going beyond a 28mm. wide angle is neither necessary nor advisable for most outdoor work.

While the wide angle is most useful—indeed I sometimes do not even carry a normal lens if weight or packing space is a factor—the telephotos are your great need in shooting pictures of wildlife. Telephoto lenses for 35mm. camera come in all lengths from about 85mm. to 1,000mm. While the smaller ones have specialized uses, the medium and long ones are the lenses that "bring in the game." There is however a definite limit, a place where you must compromise on length. Put out of your mind the idea of shooting average wildlife photos with a tripod. In the hurry and scurry afield, there is no time for tripod use. There may be times, certainly, when a tripod will be helpful and useful. But for average work, you will learn that your camera must be hand held, or placed on a gunstock type of device to assist in steadying it.

The 300mm. telephoto—which magnifies six times—is about the limit in a lens to be hand held. Lenses longer than that are too difficult to keep steady, and of course all lens movement and "shake" in your hand is exaggerated in telephotos in direct proportion to their magnifying abilities. The 300mm. is an excellent choice as a long lens, and with it if you use fast film—like High-Speed Ektachrome, as an example—you can shoot in good bright light, front lighted, at 1/250th at f/16 or 1/500th at f/11 with ample depth and get very excellent, sharp pictures. At 75 to 100 yards you will get with this lens an acceptable image of an animal the size of a deer. Smaller creatures will of course have to be closer.

Some of the newer 300mm. lenses are fully automatic. That is, they are wide open as you focus and they stop down and re-open automatically to save you the nuisance of having to focus and then manually stop down—something that in the rush of the moment you can easily forget to do, thus ruining pictures occasionally that you'll never get another chance at. I would therefore recommend an automatic 300mm. such as the Nikkor.

In addition to the 300mm.—which incidentally can double as a lens for much close-up work, too—you will want at least one, and probably two, less powerful telephotos. I've done very well with a 135mm. as an additional telephoto. This allows you to work at a fair distance from a hunter or fisherman and yet cover the scene without being a disturbance. One person, remember, always makes less disturbance than two, no matter how quiet and expert you may be as a photographer. Another excellent telephoto for all sorts of medium-distance and close-up uses is the 105-mm. At first you probably will not want both 105mm. and 135mm, and it may be a good idea to try each and see which suits you best. I have one photographer friend who uses a 105mm. incessantly, using this lens on one camera body and a 35mm. wide angle on another.

One error beginners in wildlife work often make is in trying to use a modest telephoto—such as the 105 or 135mm.—for ranges far too long. Remember, when you look at a deer at 100 yards through your 135mm. lens it may *look* like a good picture, but that's because you are actually seeing the whole big scene, brought closer about as a 2½ X telescope sight would show it. But when the scene is on a 35mm. slide, it is going to be extremely disappointing. And so, a rule of thumb particularly in the beginning is: Don't waste film by trying to stretch your lenses! Use a longer lens, or get closer.

Let me also caution you, in regard to your still camera, about zoom lenses. There are a number of these now available, and they are very tempting. They seem at first glance to offer all sorts of advantages. Some are indeed fine lenses. But zoom lenses used on still cameras are inclined to be lacking in sharpness.

Generally, a lens of a single fixed power will give better results than the finest zoom lens set to that same power.

I would suggest you use a camera with a built-in, through-the-lens meter. However, if you do not, then you will need a good meter to add to your equipment. Also useful is a so-called "spot" meter, which measures light in a small, circular area. This is for use with your more powerful lenses. For instance, if you are photographing a moose that is 100 yards away under a tree, use of the "spot" meter will give you the light reading on your shaded subject and it won't "read" the bright sunlight that may lie in between.

There is a vast amount of optional equipment that you can add. But it is really better to go as light as possible. Stick to the fundamentals. Camera "bugs" are inclined to go overboard and to get so foundered in gadgets that they stagger around missing opportunities. Certainly if you want to try for some of the very toughest shots, items like remote-control units and fast-sequence motors are not without their distinct advantages. But there are so many possibilities in that field that we cannot get deeply into them here.

I think if I had to choose just one such bit of special equipment, I'd take along a remote-firing outfit, but with nothing more complicated than a solenoid switch which would trip the shutter when I pushed a button as far away from the camera as I cared to string wire. If you try this, however, let me caution you about a mistake that is often made. (I know, because it has happened to me.) If you're working any distance from your camera, be sure you're situated so you have reference points which will allow you to determine when the game is both *in the frame* and *within the range of focus.*

Still photography is in many ways far more difficult than shooting movies. This is particularly true in amateur or hobby work. If you wish to take movies, I would suggest using one of the new Super-8 cameras. It is simple to travel with, light, versatile, easy to load. Here again, however, are decisions which "bulk" and "budget" must control. A zoom lens for a movie camera has many uses, and it does not have the inherent disadvantages mentioned for still photography. Of course, I do not mean to imply that a zoom is not the answer at times for individual use anyway. I think probably the easiest way to say it is that in all photography sooner or later the *amount* of equipment has to be limited. There are times when the drawbacks that a zoom may have are outweighed by the obvious advantage of lessening the burden.

There are so many little things one learns by experience, and these experiences pile up until you do things by instinct. For example, I never take a picture of an animal running away, that is, rear-end-on, unless I intend to use it in a sequence and for a special purpose. I try to avoid shooting creatures looking *away,* unless of course there is a specific reason why they are doing this that the picture deftly explains.

All wildlife "lives" in pictures according to its expression, by the look of its *eyes.* A photo of a wild turkey, as an example, with its head hidden behind a tree really isn't a picture at all. But one of its head peeking around the tree and its beady eye showing, alert and searching, says a great deal.

In fact, one of the great challenges in taking game pictures is trying for the picture that tells a story. Remember the old cliché about one pic-ture being worth a thousand words? The story-telling picture can be worth a thousand *dollars!* I've taken countless pictures in Africa and granted many have been taken before. But in an effort to bring them above the norm, I have constantly sought artistic light, exceptional angles, unusual backgrounds, and any other attributes that might improve quality and make an otherwise so-so picture striking. What will turn the trick better than any other single device is to catch animals *doing something interesting.*

Once, for example, I was shooting what I felt were rather exceptional pictures of a group of lions just lounging around. As I was taking these pictures, a rhino appeared, coming over a low hill. It seemed half ugly and it walked straight to the lions and began to disturb them. It reminded me of a mean kid on a beach just pestering sunbathers out of pure devilishness. And what a series this made! Now the animals were no longer lounging. Something was happening. The rhino's actions, and the snarling expressions of the lions, told a story that was priceless.

I will readily admit that luck played a most important part in getting such a set of pictures. Many professionals dislike crediting luck. But where wildlife photography is concerned, certainly luck can be important. However, it is still the man with the camera who must be ready to seize the opportunity. Having proper equipment, and keeping it handy and ready at all times often *makes* one's own luck. Many great shots are missed because a cameraman is "unarmed" at the crucial moment.

Many small things that sound awfully obvious have to be learned and relearned. One is: always carry *plenty* of film. Not only on a whole trip, but in your pocket or on your person somewhere, every minute. How many times I have been lured to stalk some creature, have shot and shot—and then just as I am out of film and reminded that I do not have a spare roll on my person, the animal poses beautifully and I have to stand there in complete frustration.

Another constant item to bear in mind is to mother your film and equipment like an old hen. Heat and dampness are mortal enemies even of today's nearly indestructible film. Dust and too-rough use can maim cameras so that when the crucial shots show up, you are out of business. I've found the best thing to carry equipment in is a dustproof, foam-lined case, preferably made of light metal. But these shine badly and can scare wildlife, so I cover the hinges and locks with masking tape, then spray the case dull green with a few spots of brown for camouflage.

This gets us to the value of camouflage, and getting close to game. Lengths of camouflage mosquito netting can be bought as war surplus, or from firms making camouflage clothing for hunters. These are light and extremely useful for quickly covering up a shiny tripod, or the photographer himself. Animals coming to a waterhole or salt lick (good spots to catch them with your lens) are wary. Danger always lurks at such places. Animals know this instinctively. They check carefully with their keen eyes before coming close. Camouflage clothing and a headnet and even net camouflage gloves can be most useful.

The comparatively pale human face and hands are sure panic for wild creatures. You can get in a habit of simply wearing full camouflage clothing on your "shooting" forays, and carrying a headnet and gloves in your pocket for specific uses. A little trick I have learned is to take along some rubber bands in varying lengths. I have them on my wrist. When I cover camera or tripod or other equipment with camouflage, I snap on a few bands. This keeps the camo net from flapping. Such unnatural movement, even of camouflage cloth, can spook an animal.

In making a stalk to get close to game, you must be ingenious. Well camouflaged as above, and sitting in a floating tube such as wading fishermen sometimes use, you can actually float with care almost in among waterfowl. Slow, patient movement on foot can put you in camera range of animals as nervous as whitetail deer. But you must recognize that all hoofed and horned games uses the sense of smell as its greatest defense. You *must* stalk into the wind.

This means you must consider how the light is, too, in relation to wind. If you make stalks on big-game animals in late afternoon, and select a day and place where any breeze is in your face but the sun at your back, you place the game at a distinct disadvantage. Bright low sun in its eyes makes seeing danger just as difficult for the animal as sun in your eyes would.

You must learn, to become expert, all sorts of facts about your subjects. Deer, for example, do not see colors as humans do, because they have no cones in the eye. But birds, like the wild turkey, that have no appreciable sense of smell, have awesomely keen eyesight, and they see colors vividly. If you stand immobile, a deer may look at you and never see you, or at least not know what you are. But move and it will flee. Its eyesight is actually very little more acute than yours.

But its hearing is far better than yours, and its sense of smell is superb. Learn signals of animals. A whitetail deer, for example, will raise its head from feeding, stare nervously all about. Perhaps it is staring at you, and you've been caught in a most uncomfortable, mid-stride position. Hold that pose! But when you see this whitetail deer give its tail a little switch, that is the "all clear." It will immediately drop its head, start to feed, satisfied momentarily that all is well. Now you can move once more.

Never skylight yourself as you stalk game. Never cross an opening if you can follow the edges. In low light, watch your long shadow. It may give you away while you think you are hidden. Your reflection in a waterhole may do the same; check on it before you hunker in your blind. An antelope, lowering its head to drink, may be staring right at you! Antelope, incidentally, and a few other animals, can be brought close by their innate curiosity at times. I've tried successfully lying on the open plain, waving my hat. A buck antelope, not knowing what this was, came well within camera range to investigate. Caribou are just as curious.

All sorts of animal and bird calls are priceless in getting you near—or rather bringing the subject near you. But you must learn how to use them with expertness. And you must study the habits and daily routines of the wildlife you hope to photograph.

We come at last to that part of good outdoor picture taking that is hardest of all for the amateur to adopt. Put simply, it is this: *The time to take pictures is right now.* Not five minutes later, when all the action has died down, or the game has drifted away. Not tomorrow, when the light may be bad—not even just "later." *The* moment when that buck pauses for a last backward look, when the sun backlights a friend casting—these are the great scenes that seldom come twice.

How do you bring yourself to do this when the fish are biting or the birds flying or whatever? Try catching *one* fish or shooting at *one* bird, then grab your camera for the *next* fish someone catches, or the *next* bird that flies. You'll miss a little personal action, sure, but if you want memorable pictures this is the guaranteed way to get them.

It is easy to see that wildlife photography is a vast and intricate subject. But it is one of the most intriguing subjects and hobbies—even careers—on earth. If you pursue it, you'll know agonizing frustration and occasionally great joy. For let nobody kid you, bringing back spooky game or a scene of great and exciting action on film takes some doing. It's a challenge that more sportsmen are discovering every year and if you take it up this season— good shooting!

**Above, Bob Halmi waits patiently in his thicket blind**

**for pictures such as the following: Below, bathing hippo**

**in Mozambique. Opposite, groaning lion in Tanzania.**

Left, Nebraska, mule deer seconds after
arrow struck it. Opposite top, cheetah in
Kenya; bottom, jaguar in British Honduras.

Left, itching zebra in Kenya;

below, hungry Kenya lions.

Opposite, elephant in Mozambique sunset.

Right, vulture and
below, white rhino
in northern Kenya.